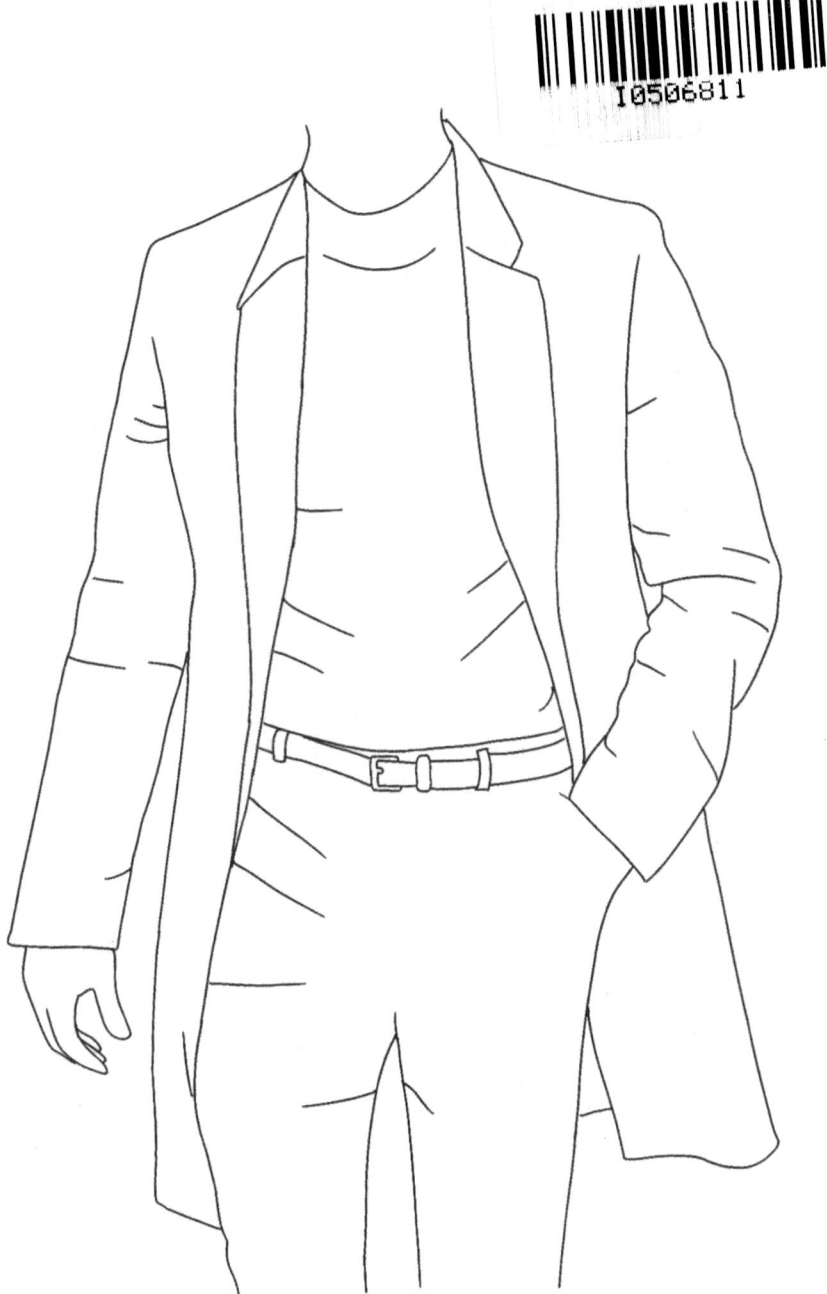

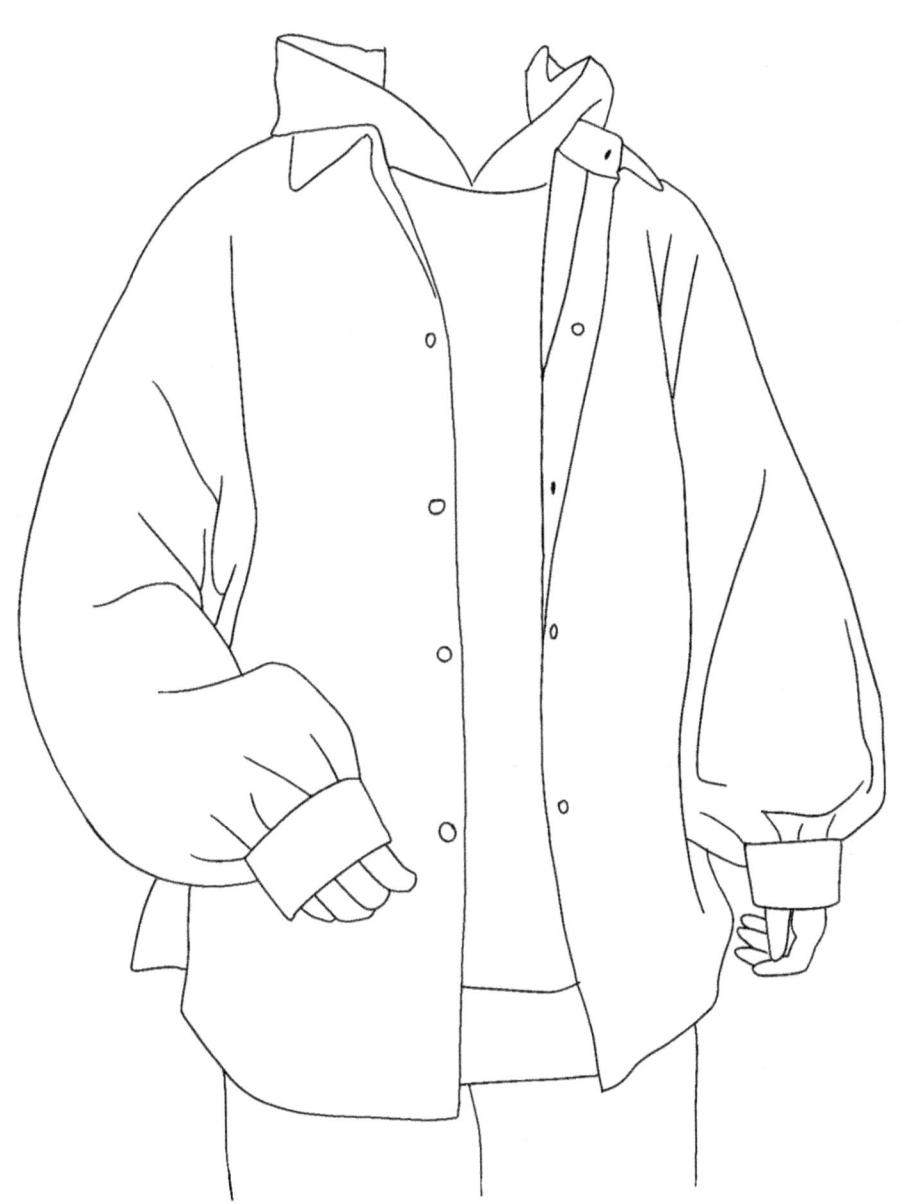

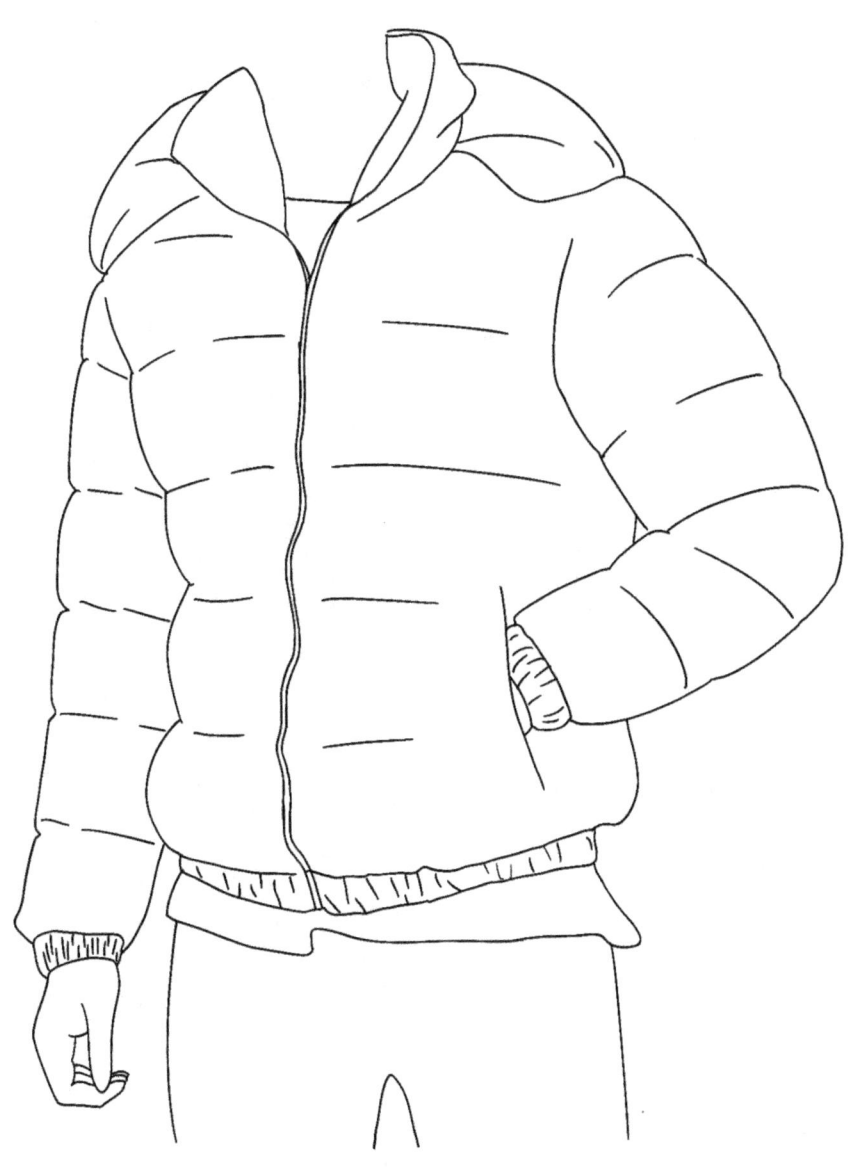

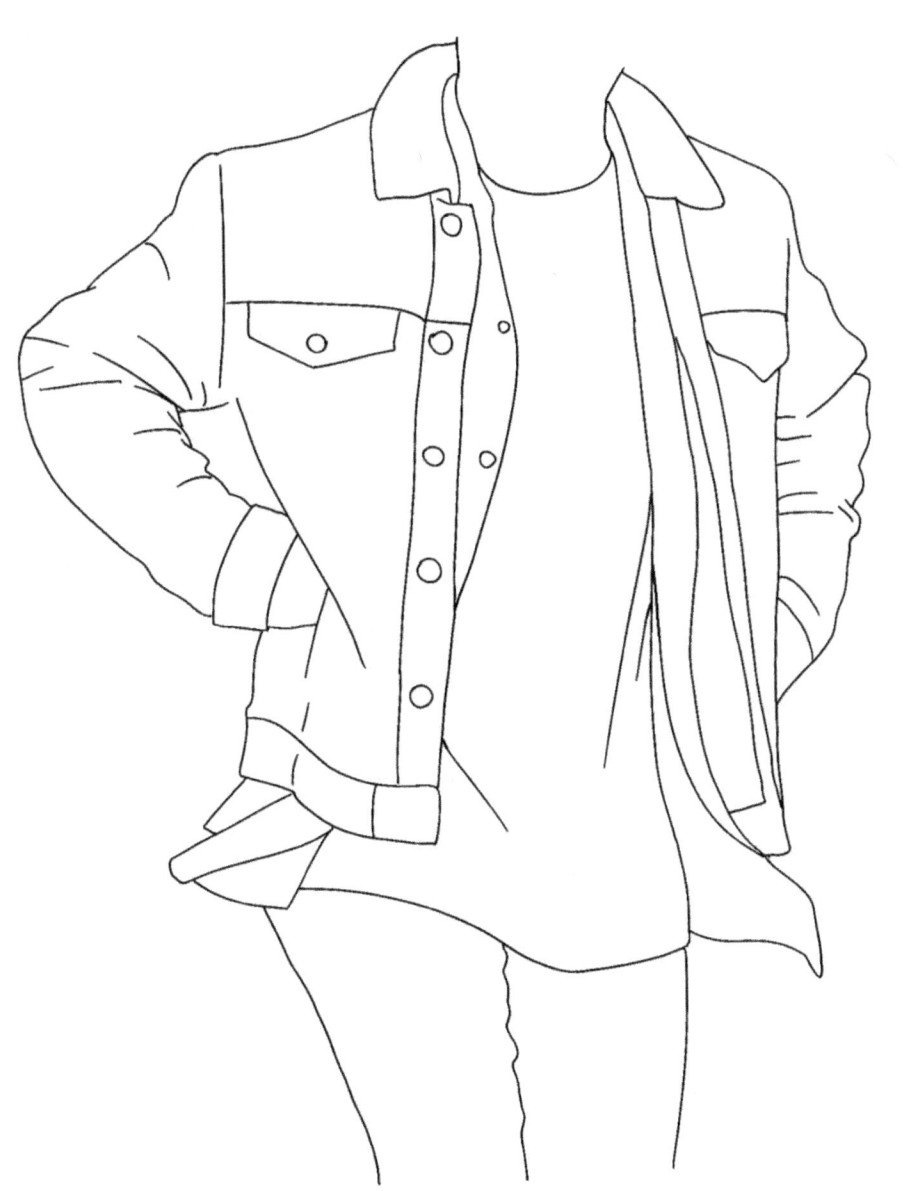

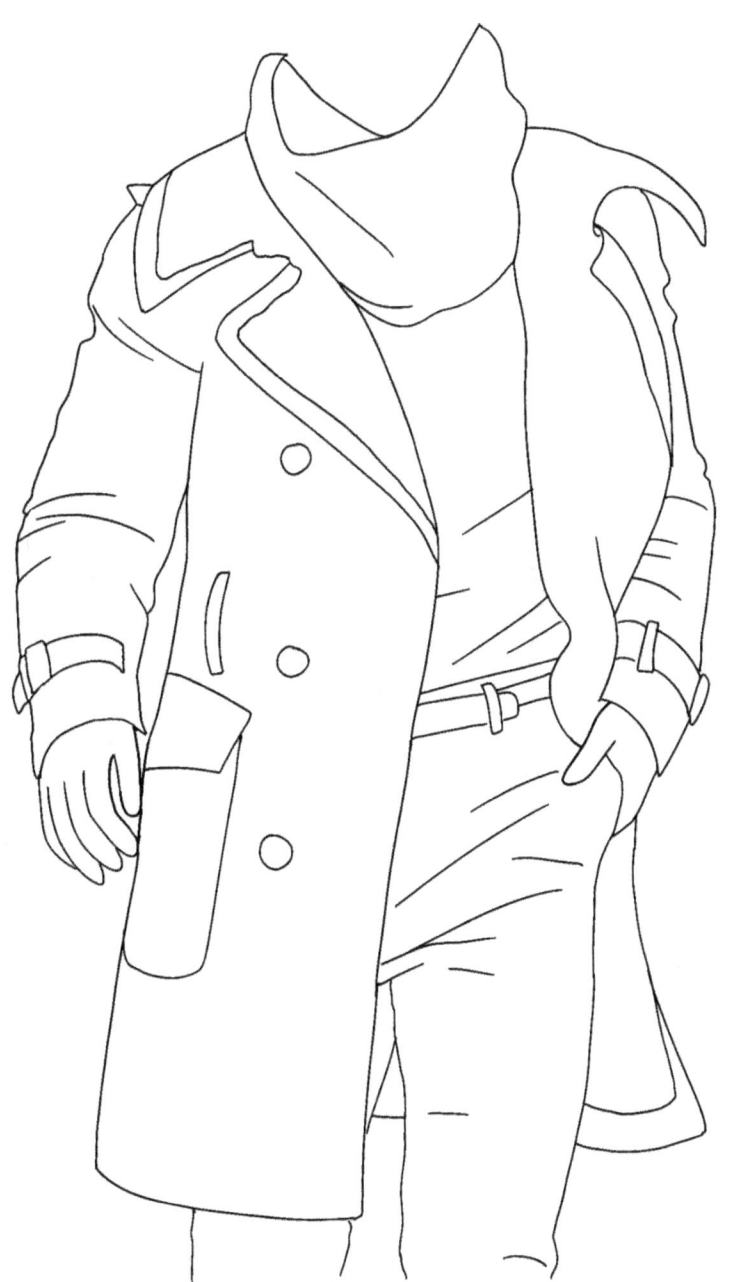

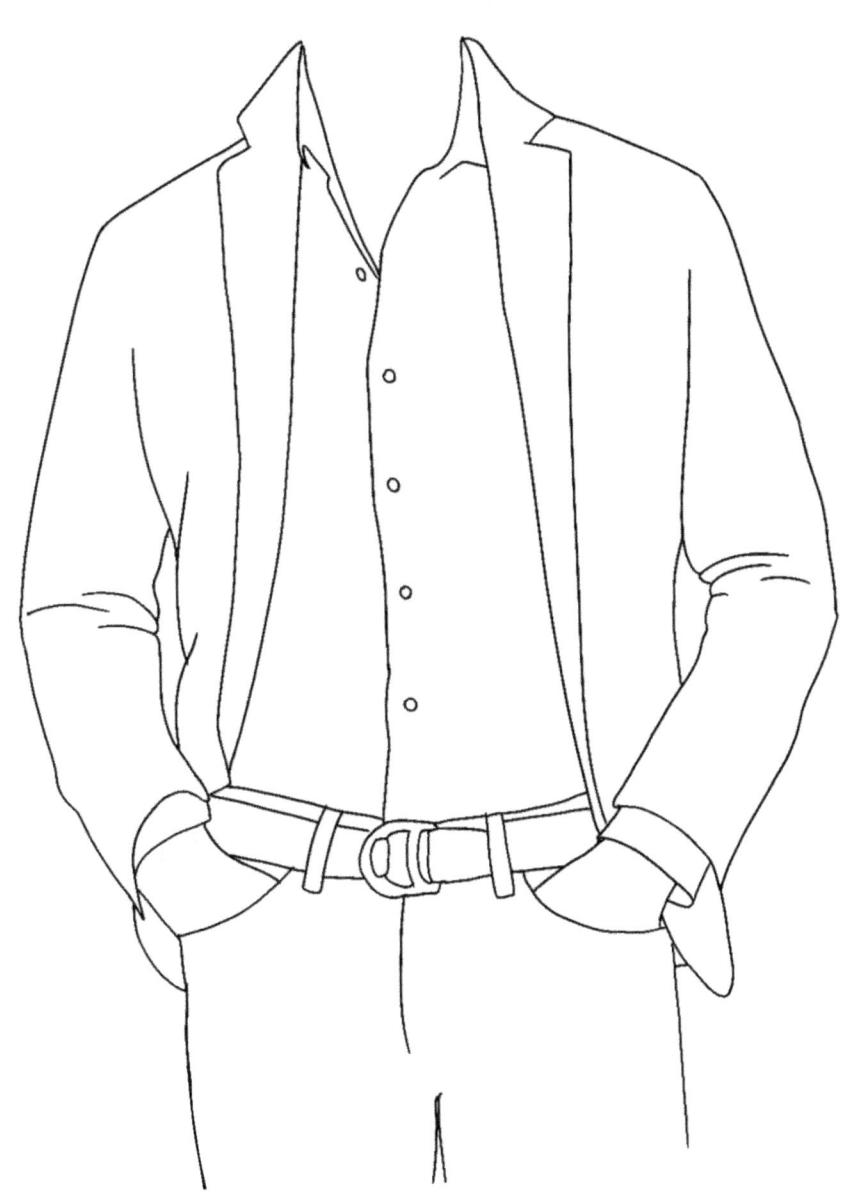

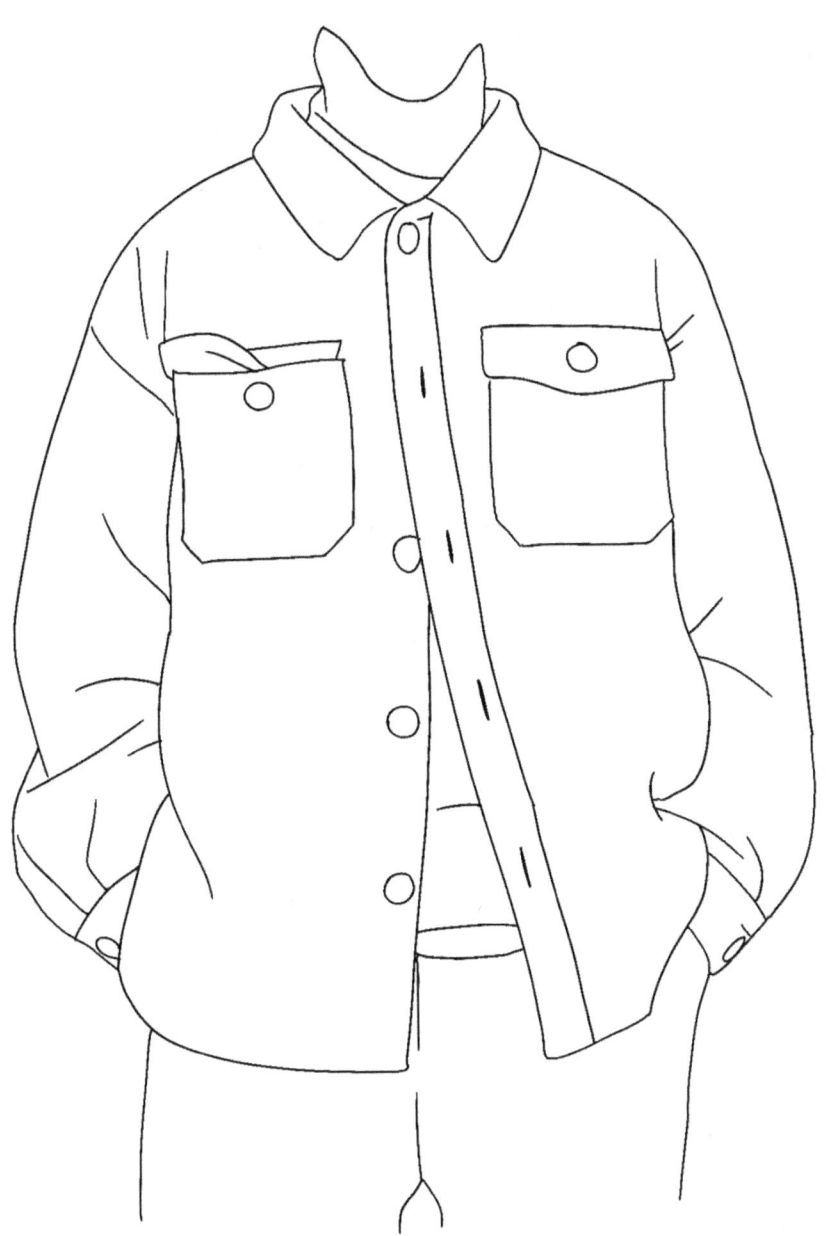

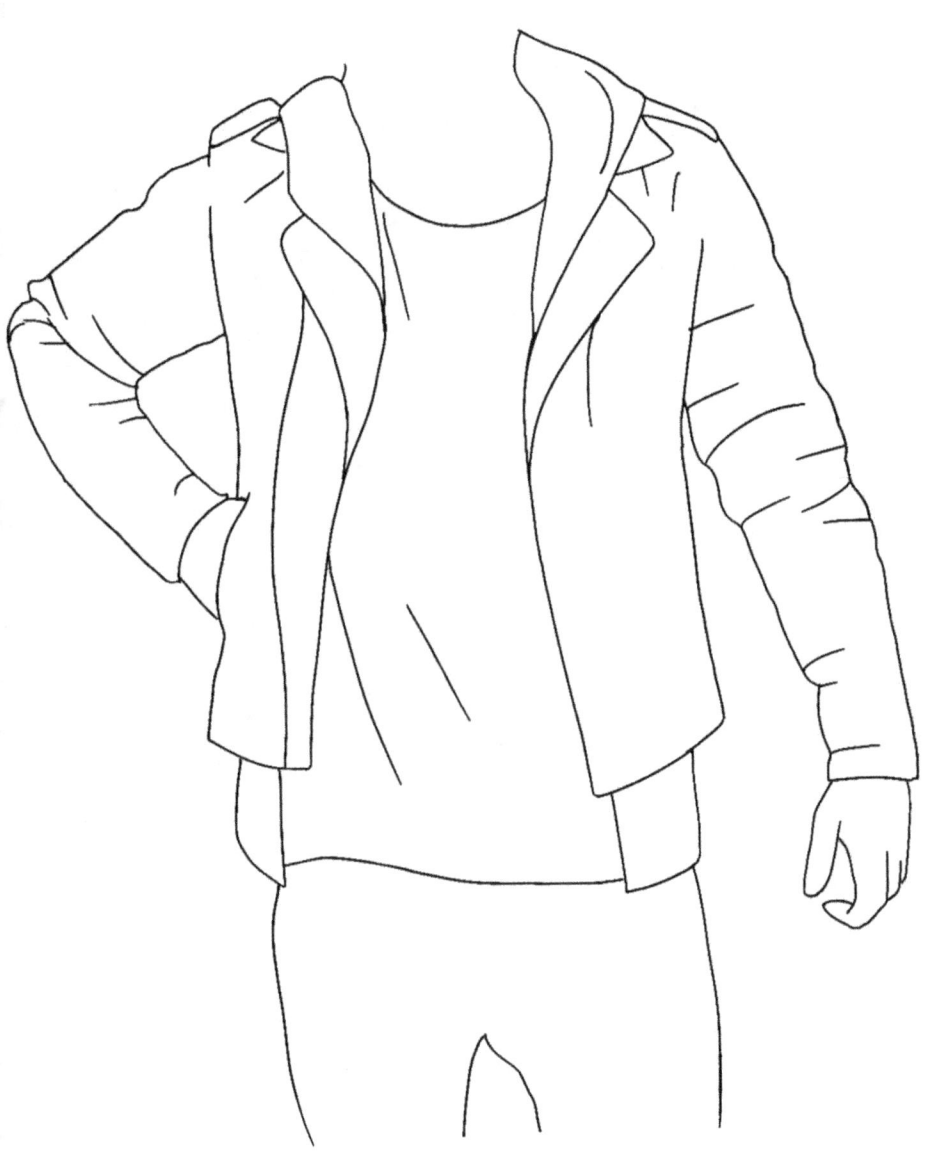

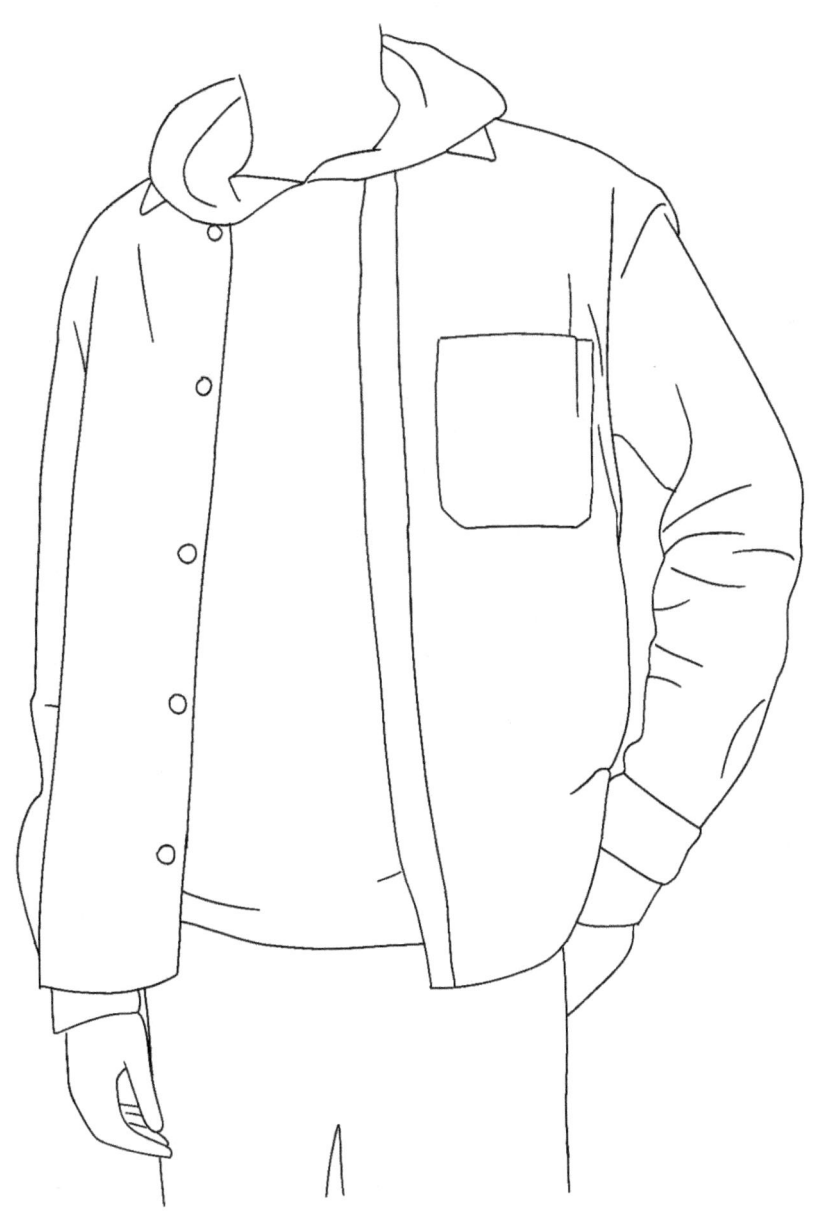

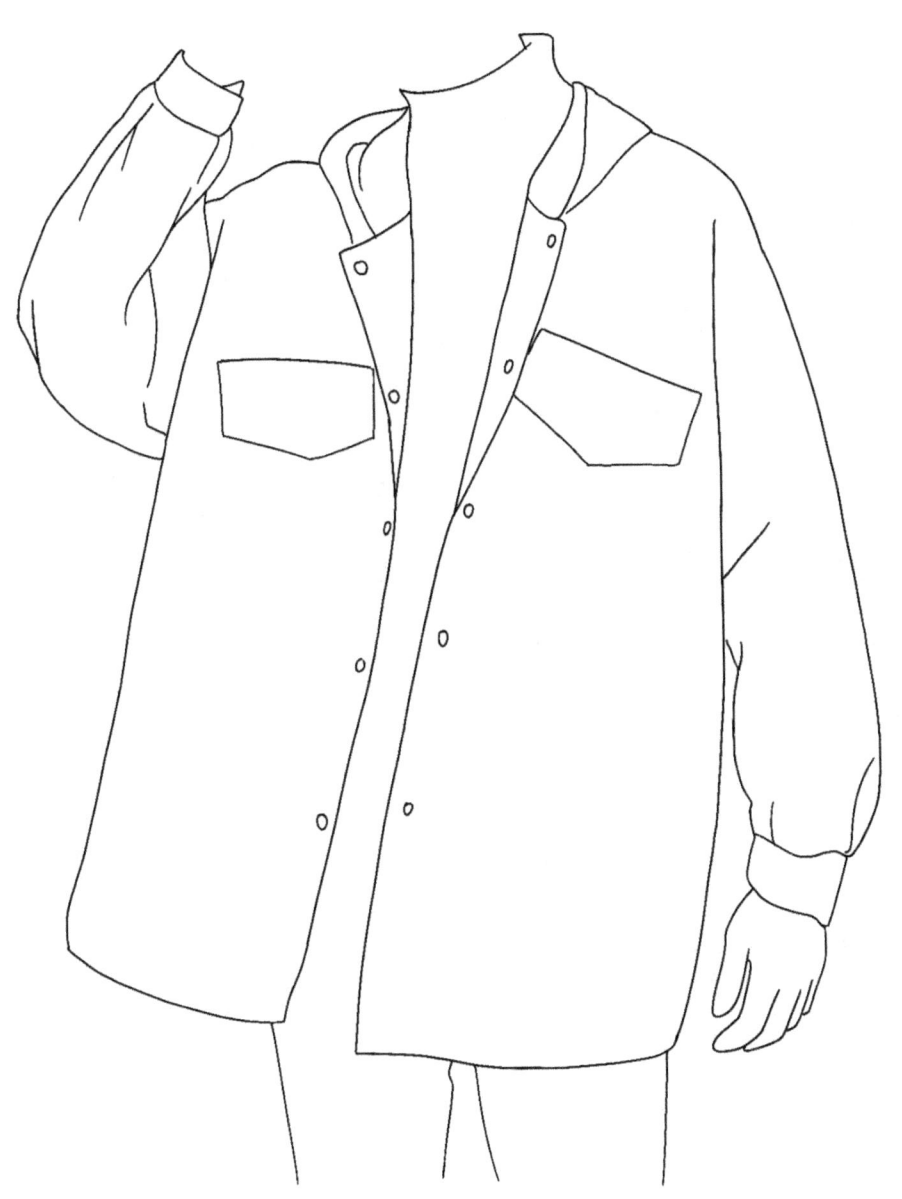

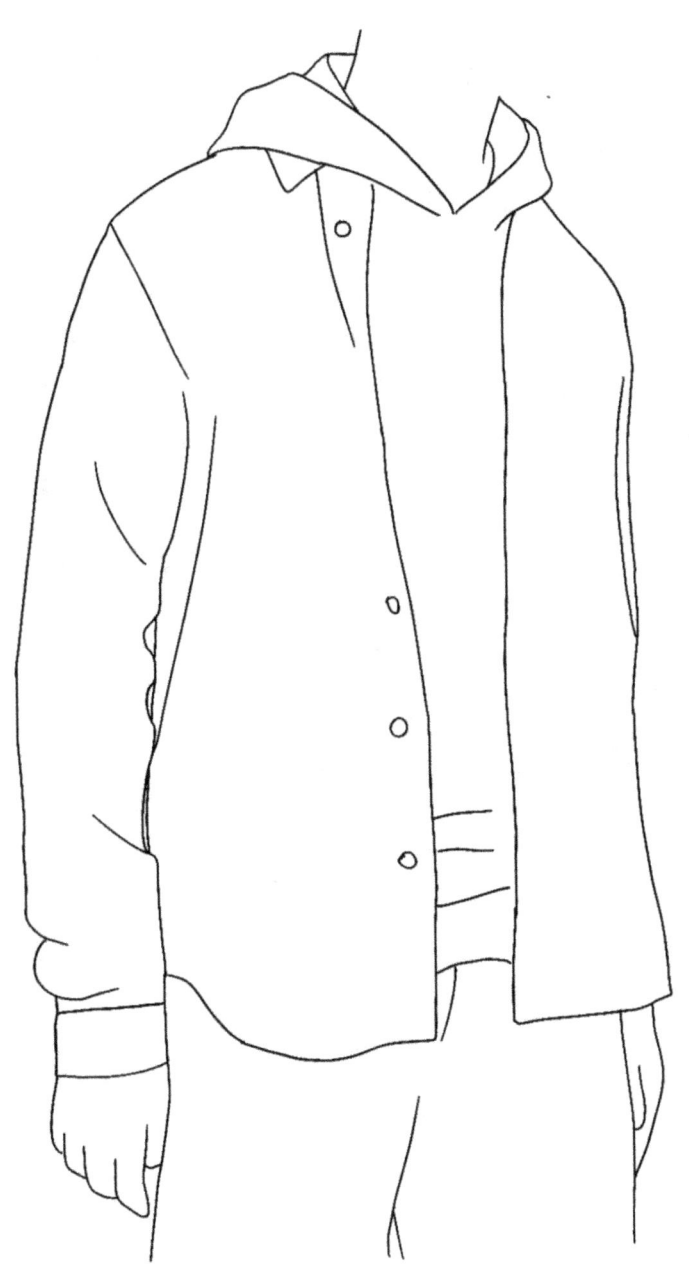

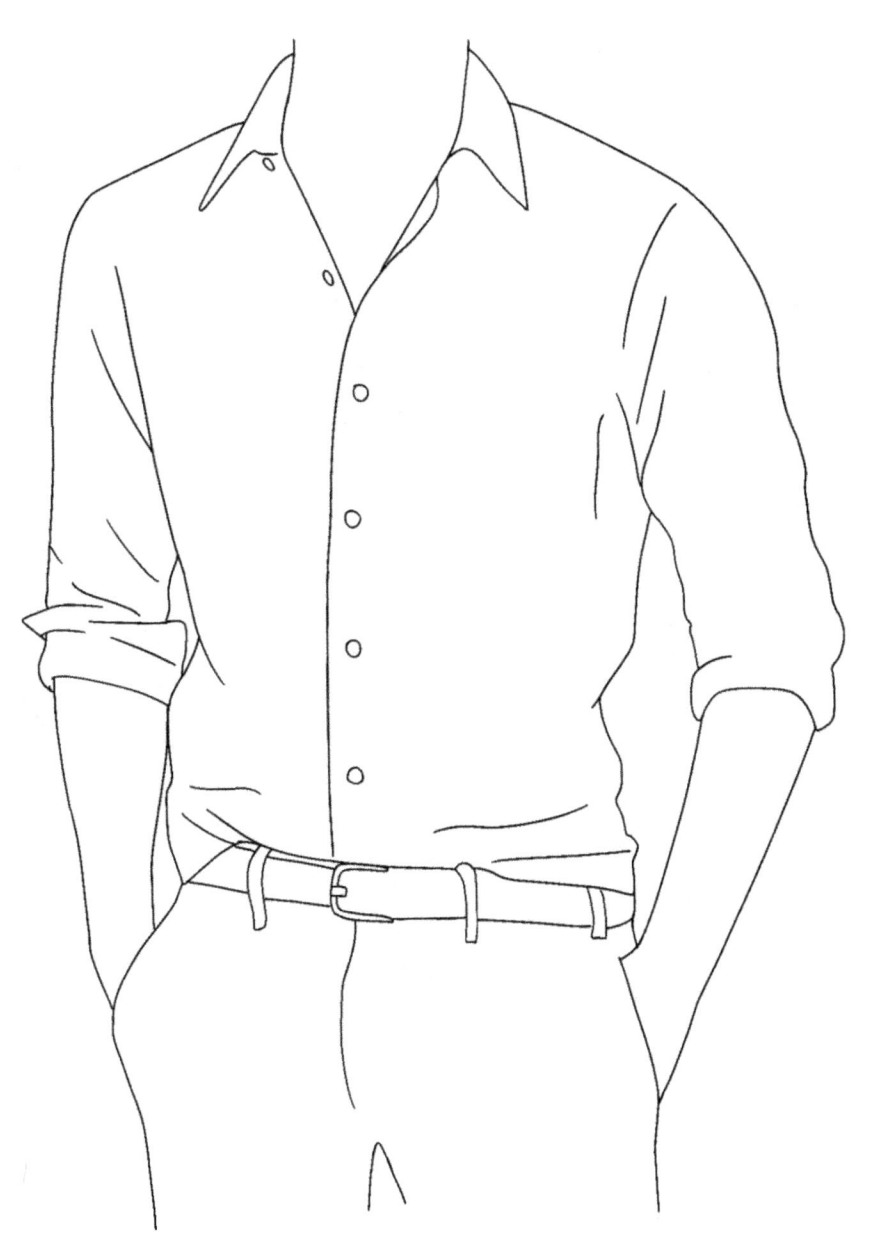

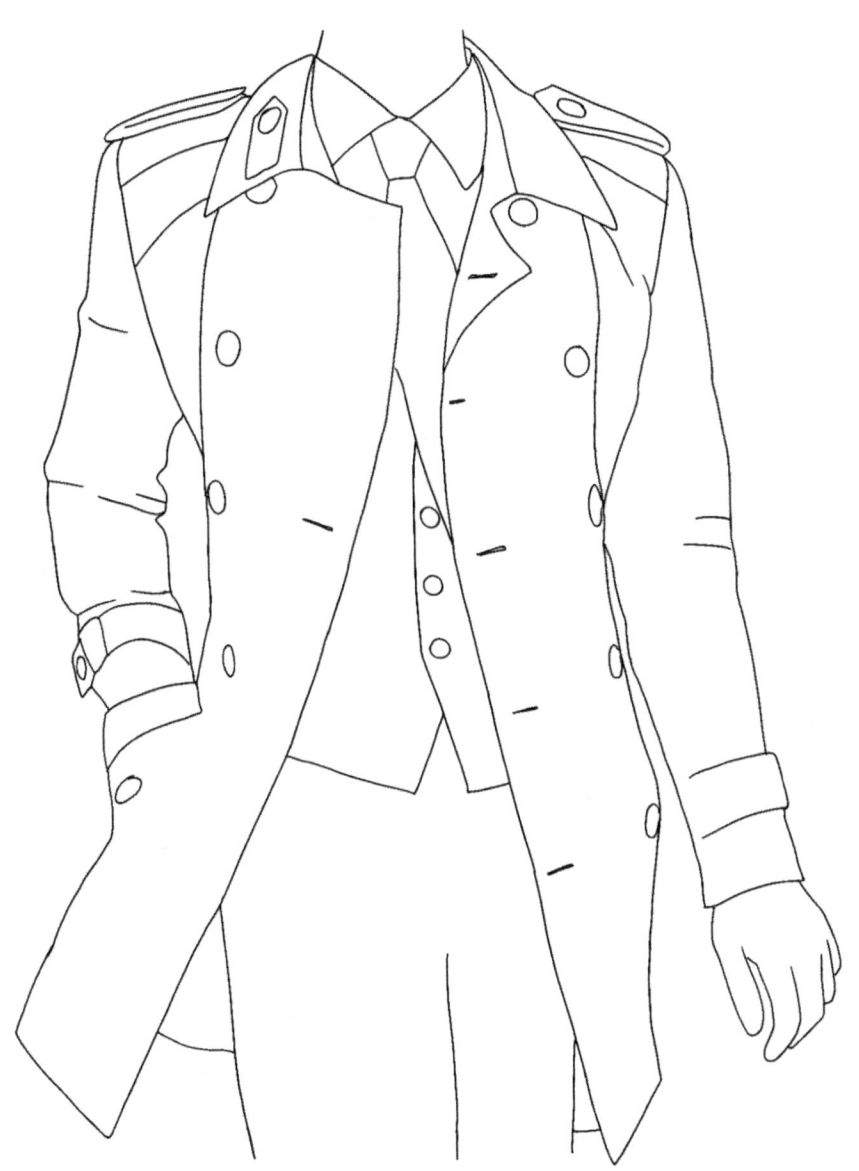

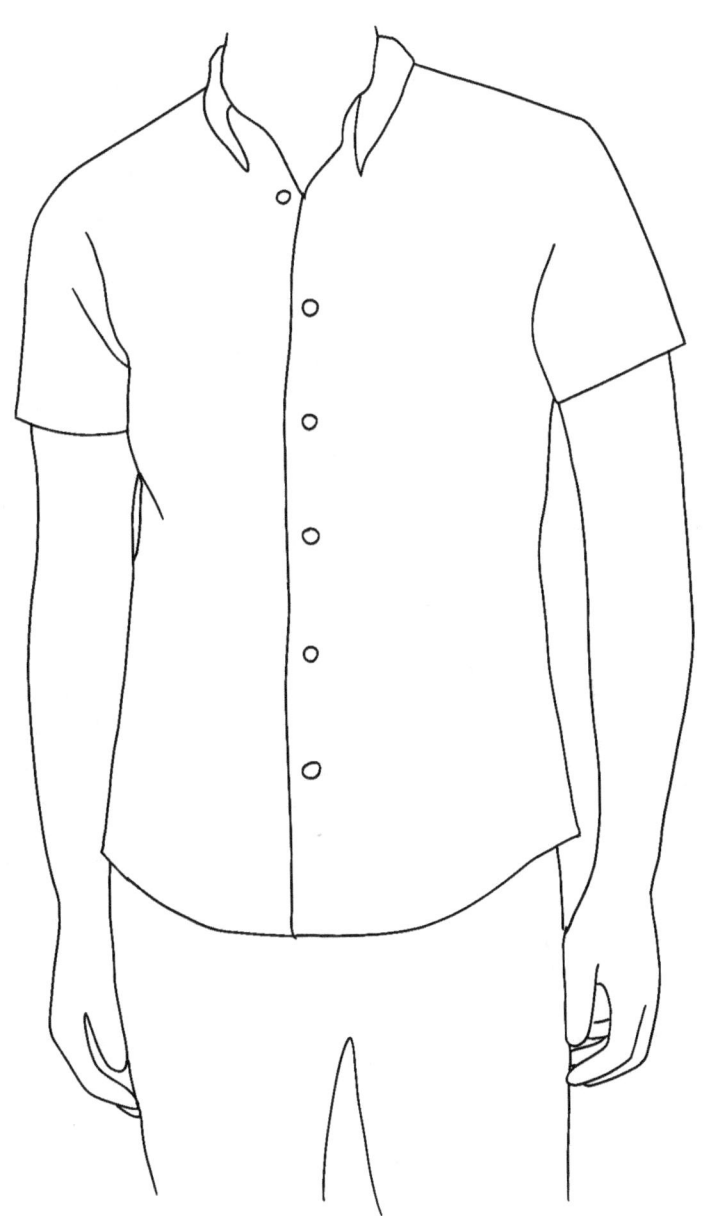

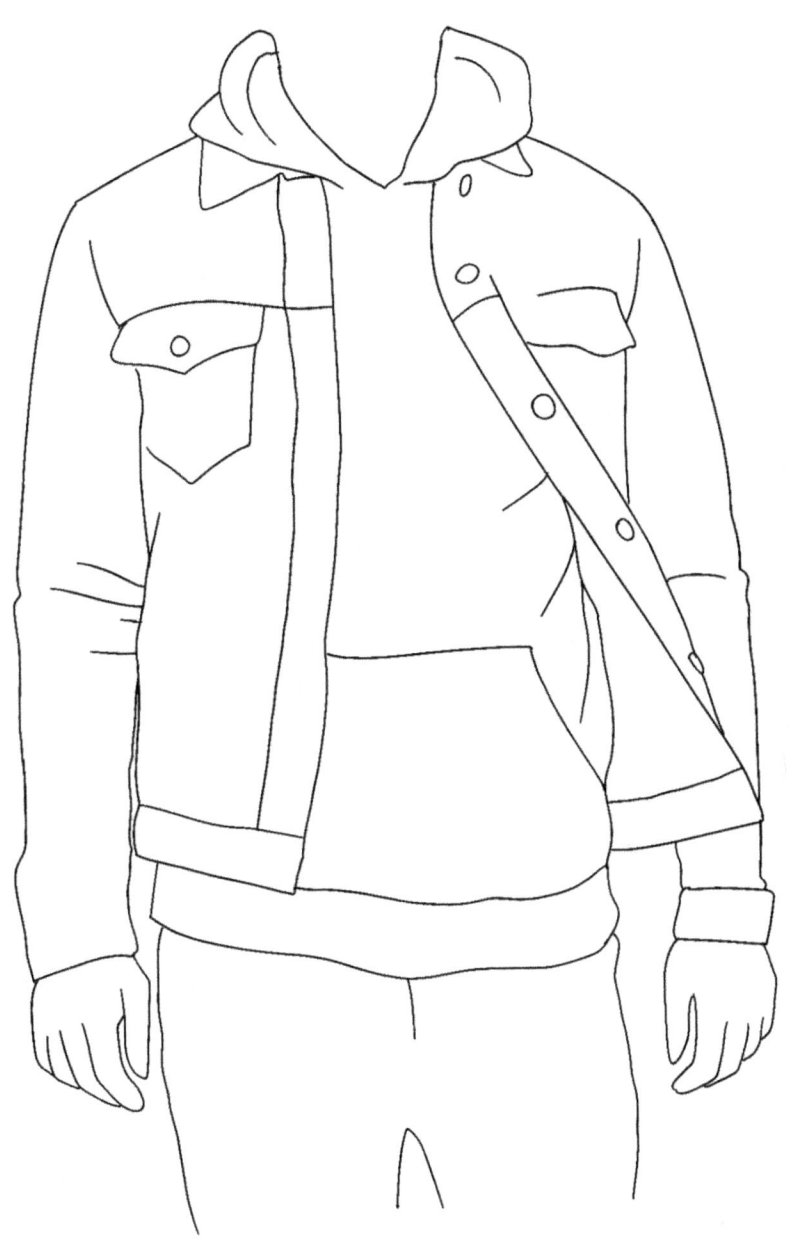

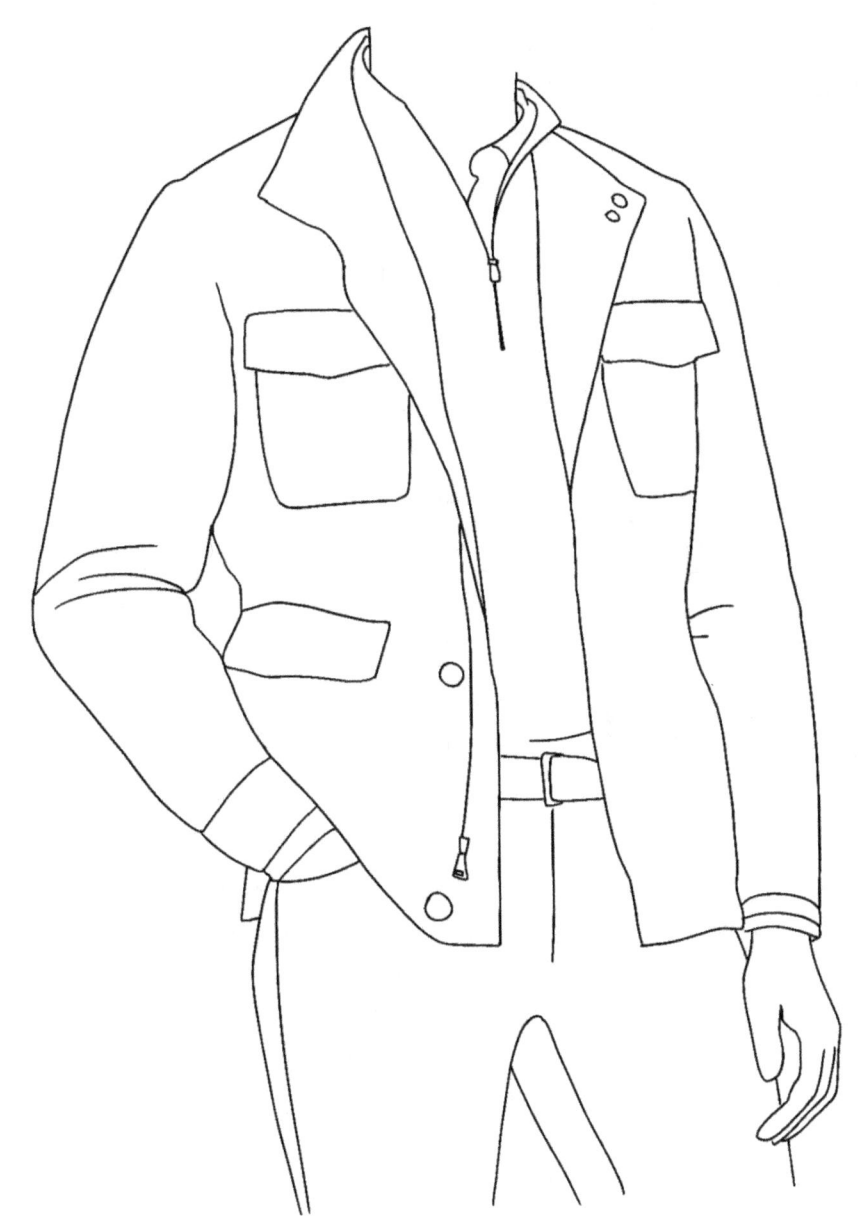

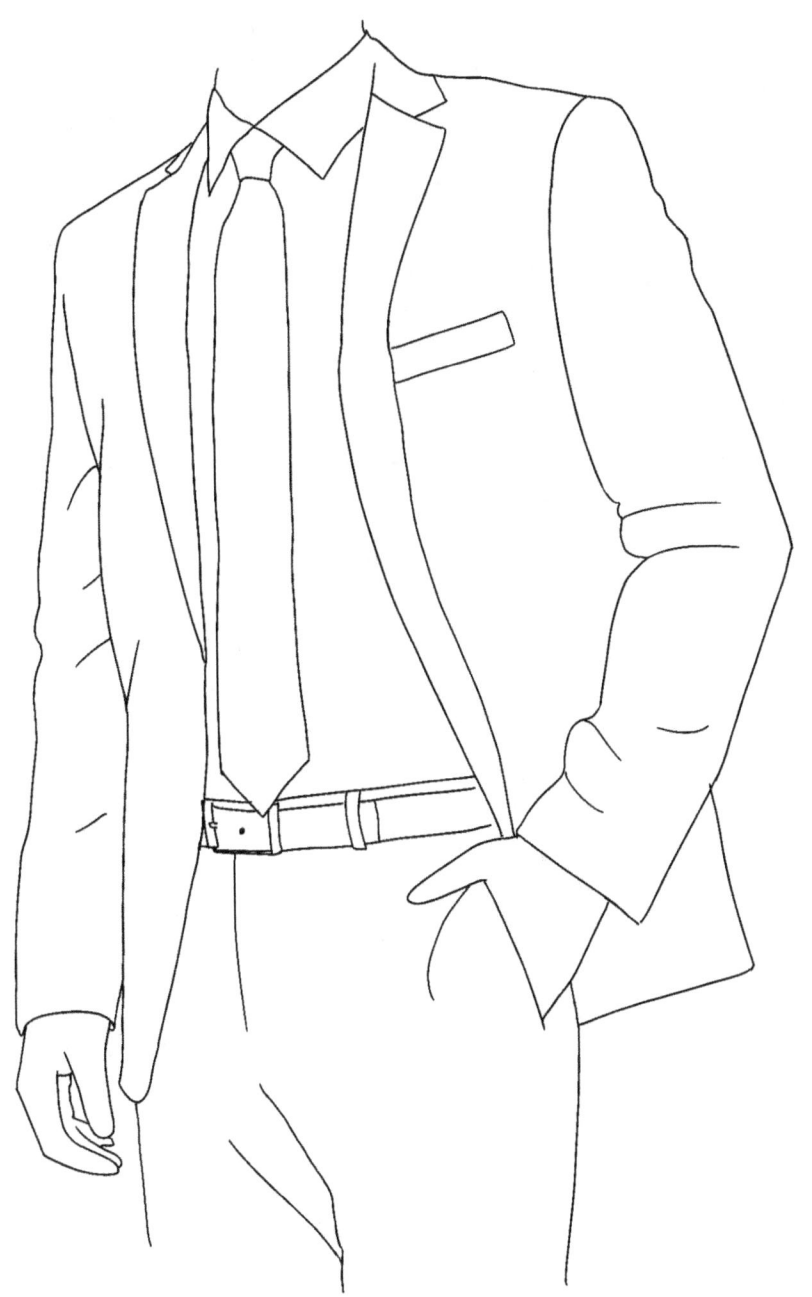

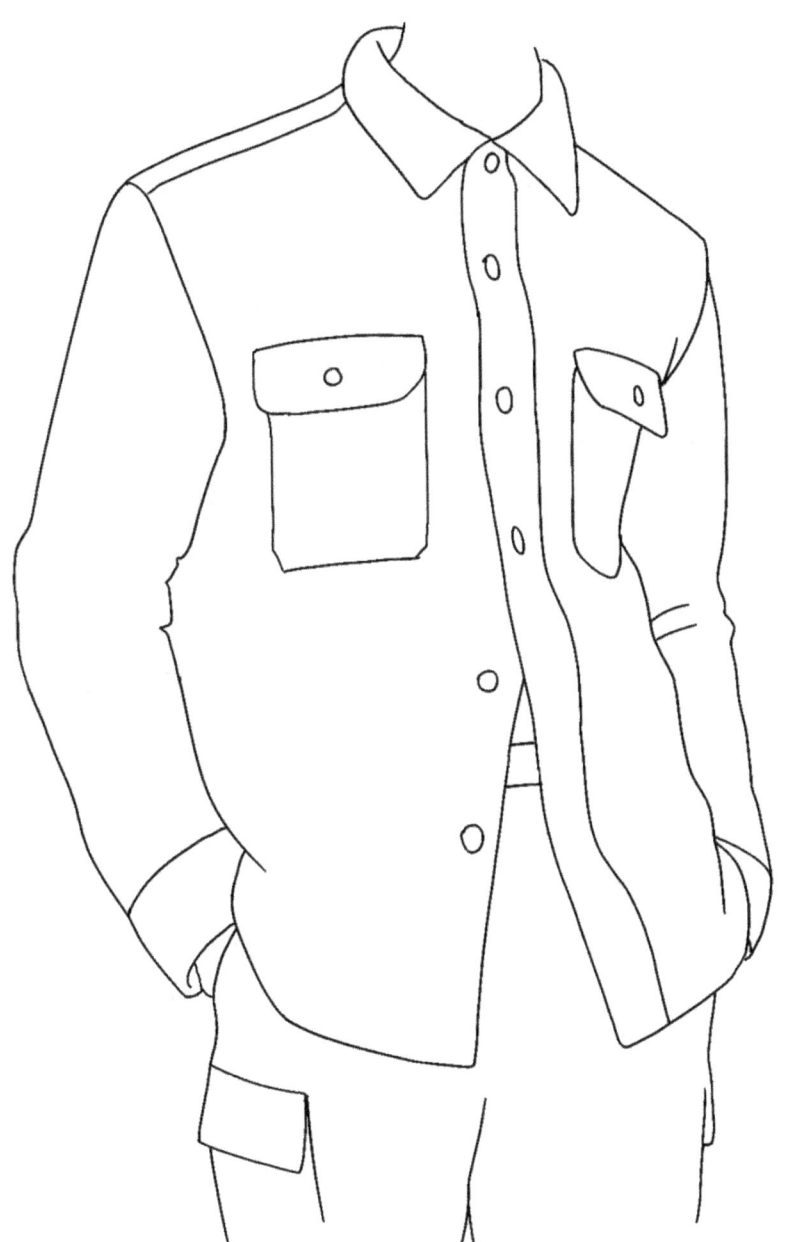

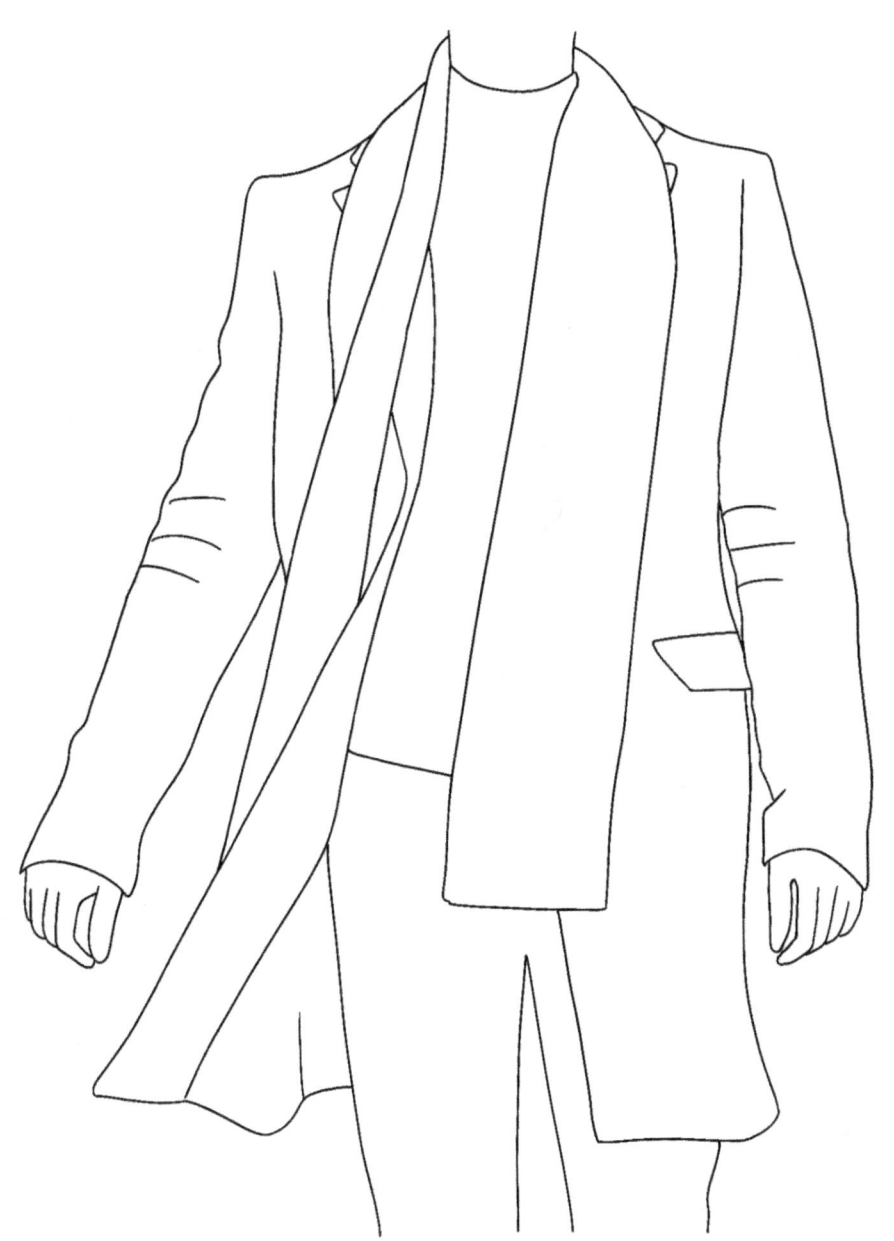

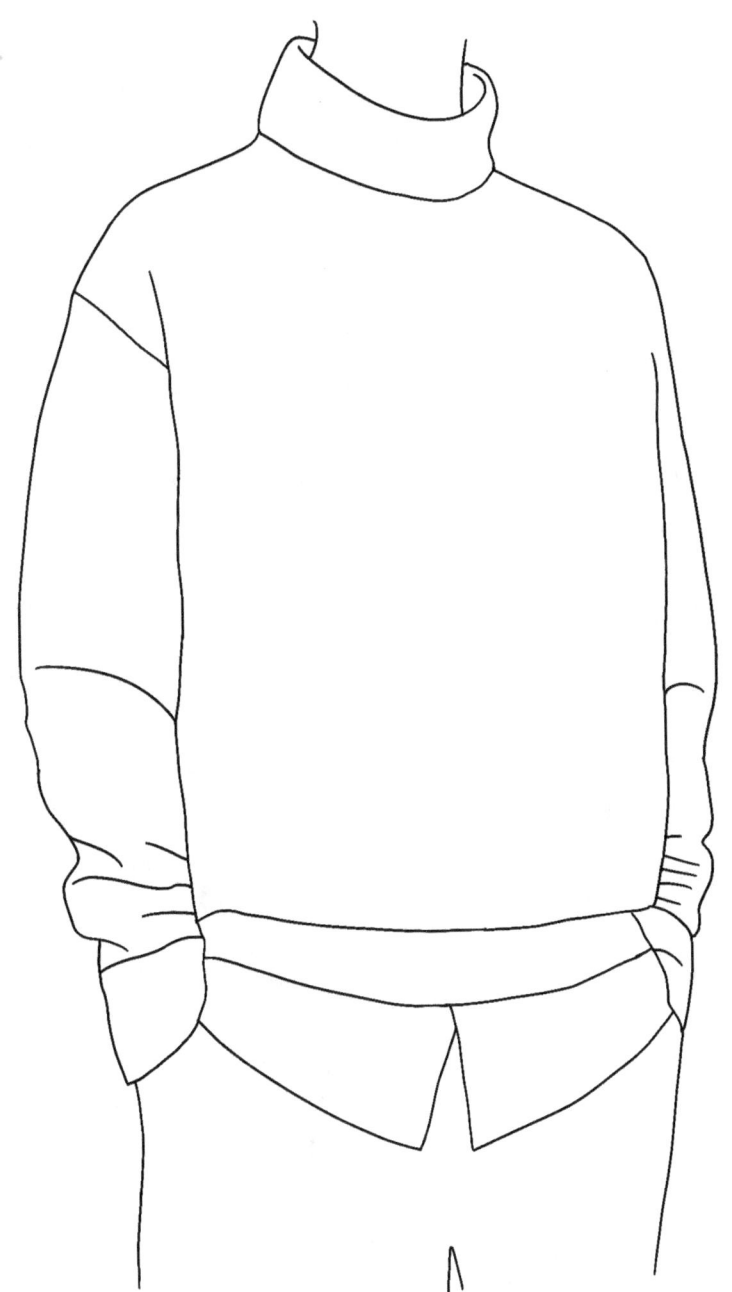

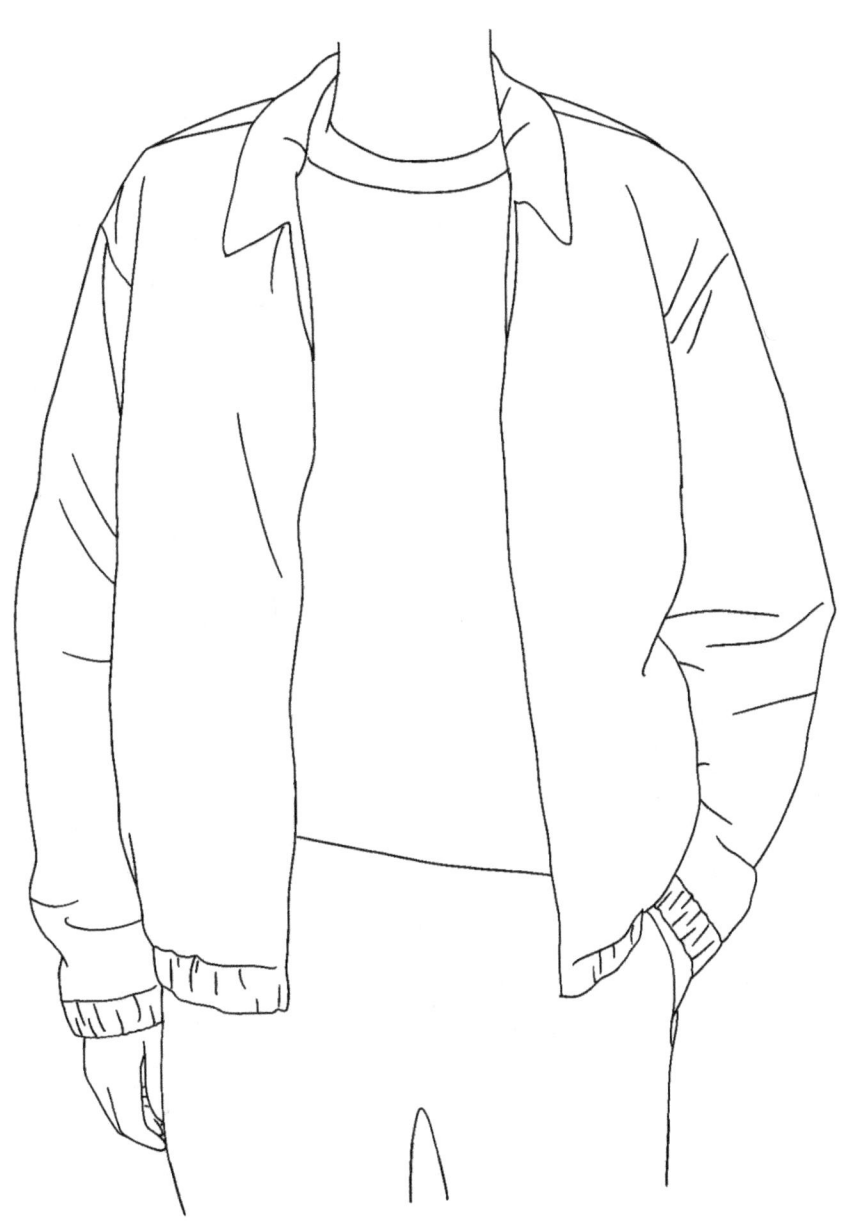

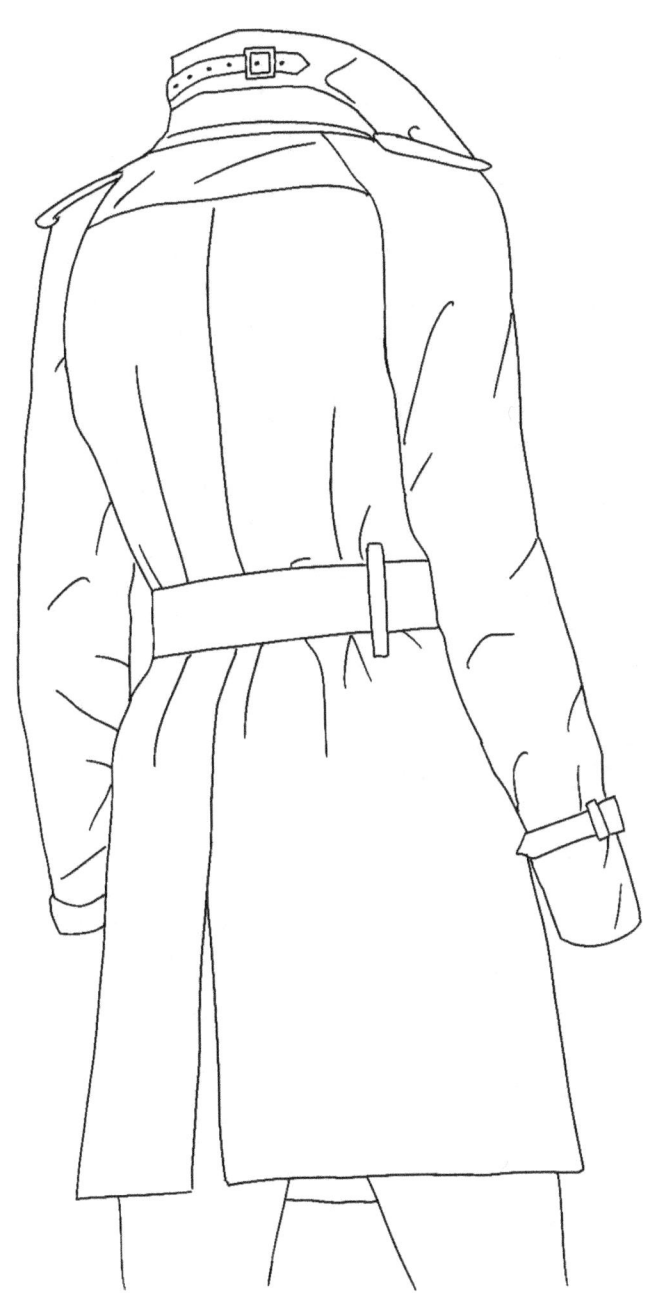

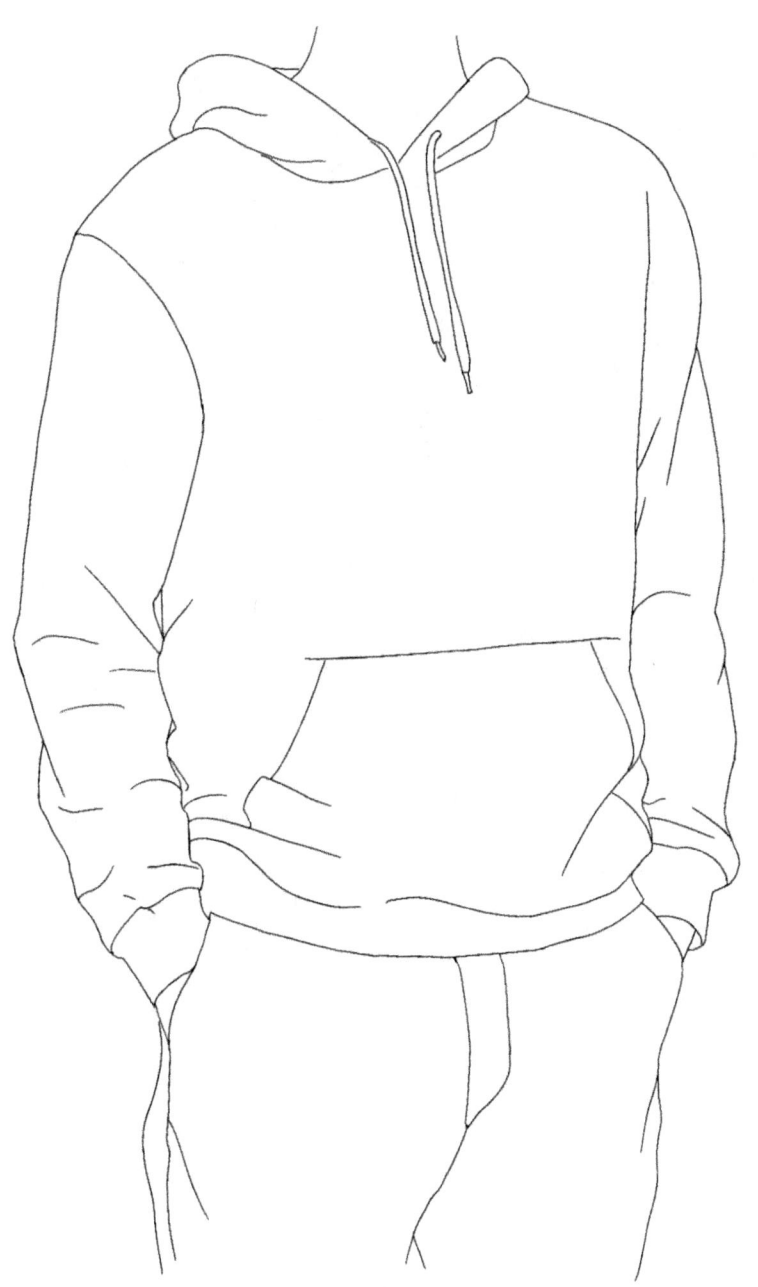

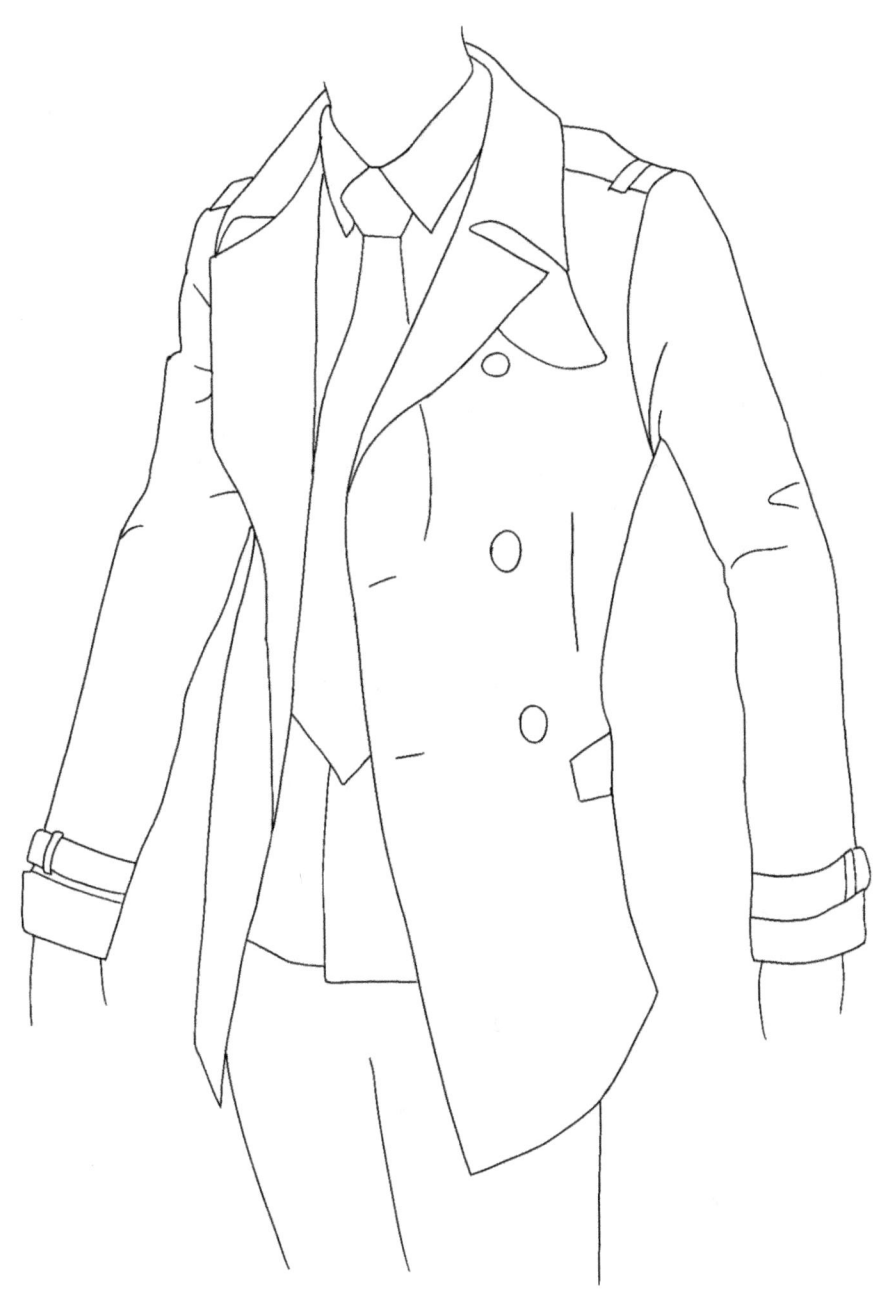

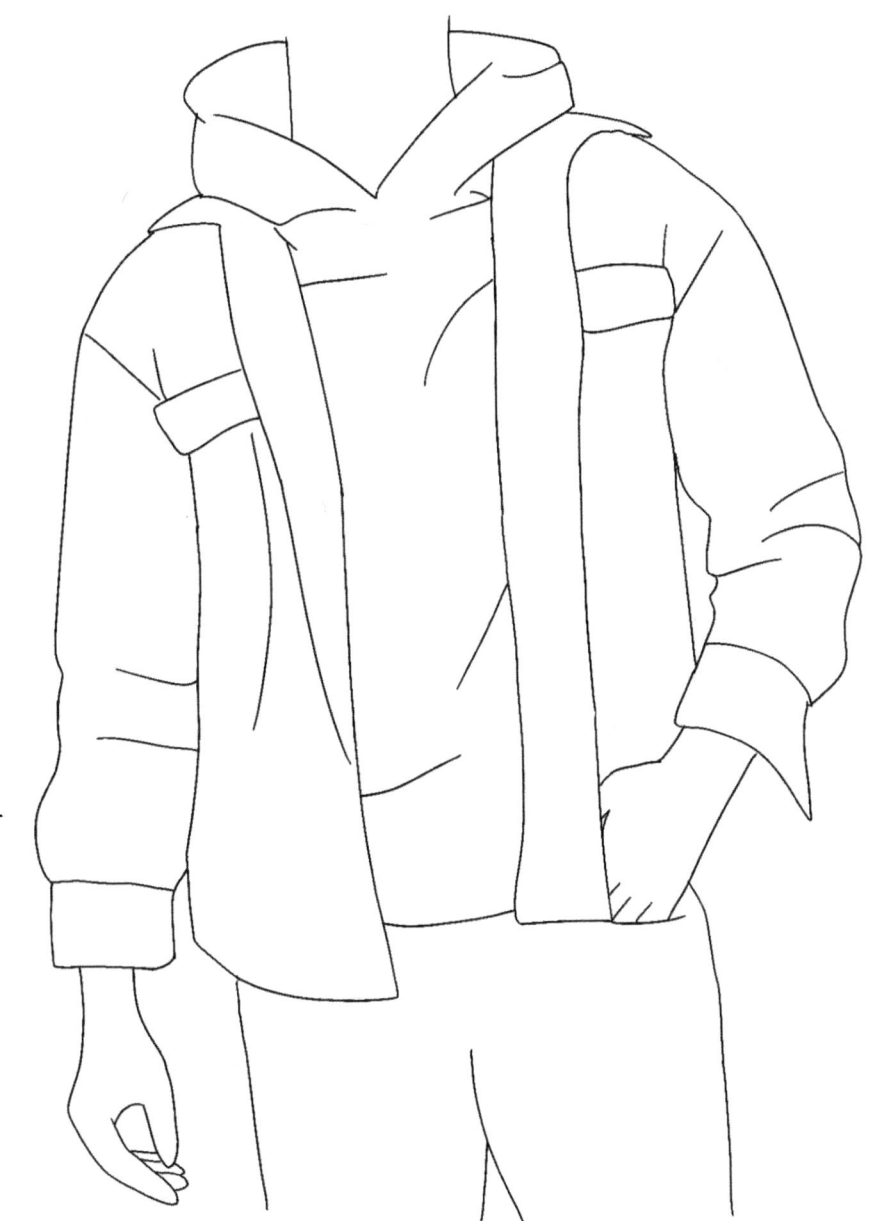

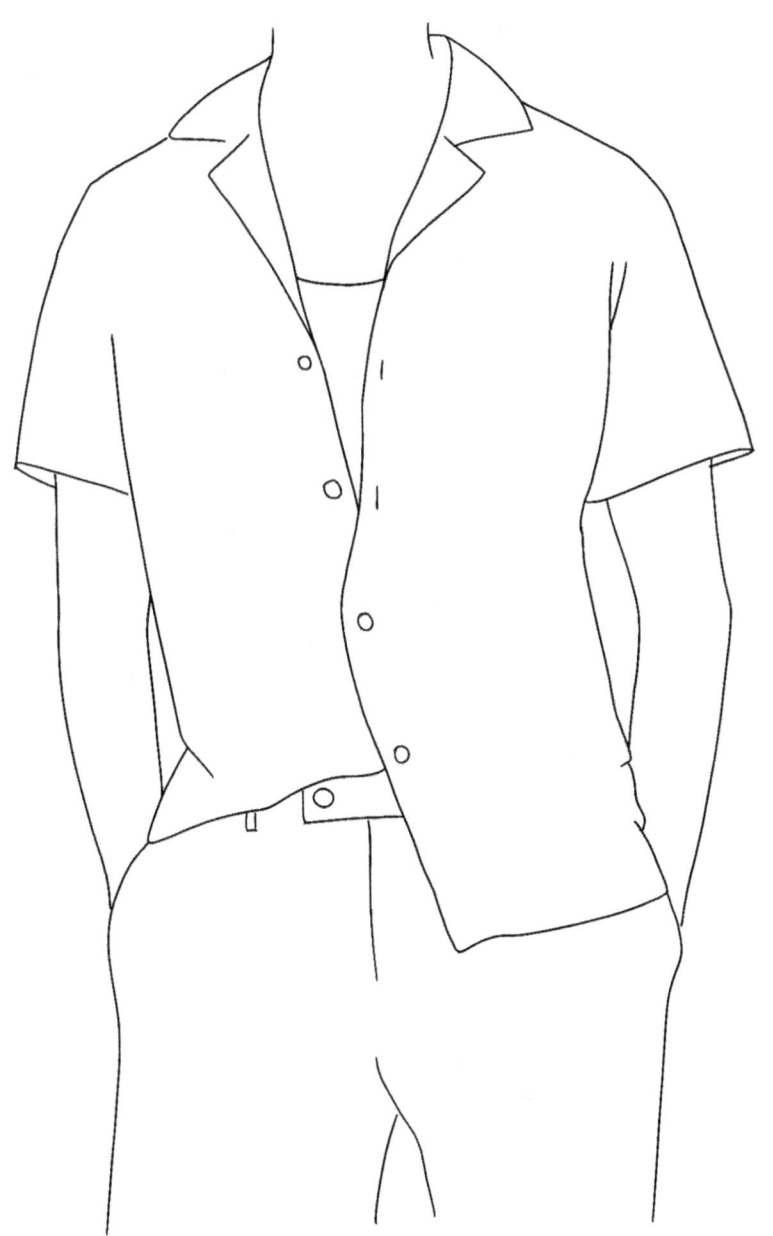

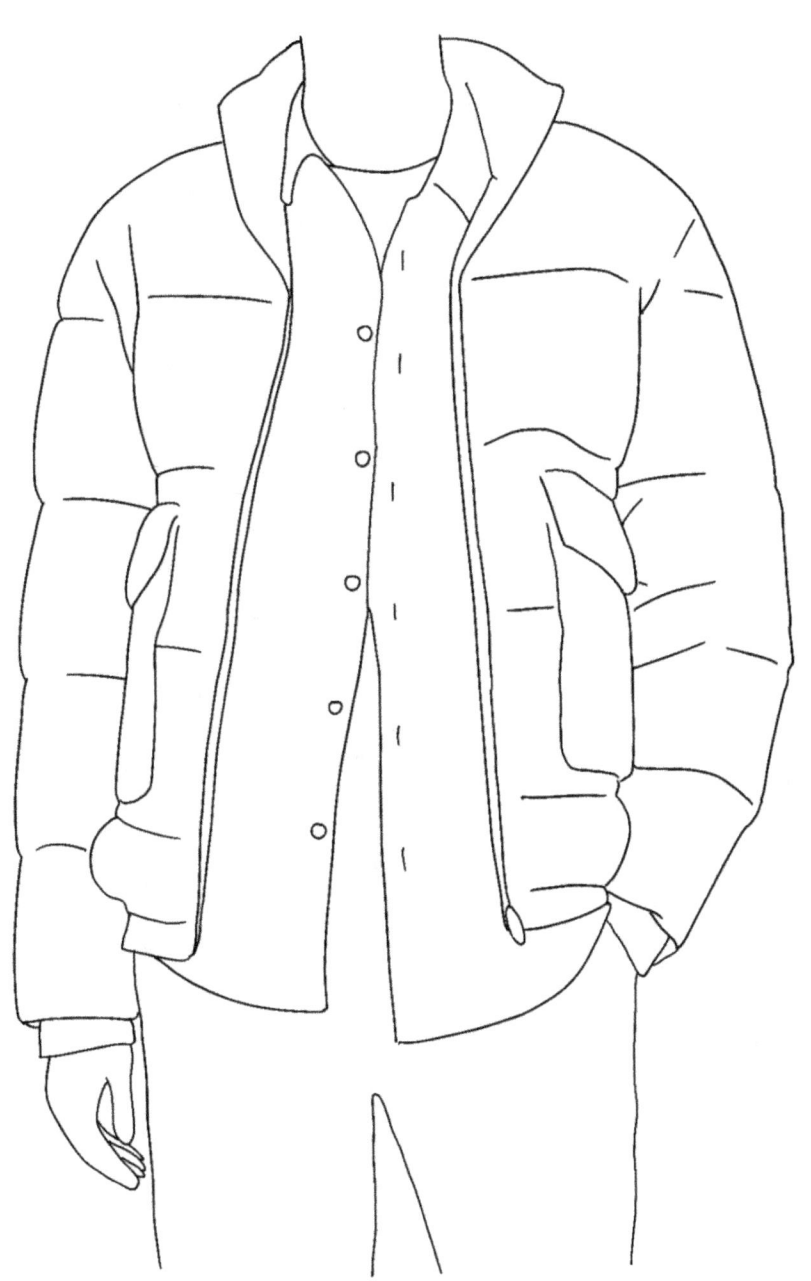

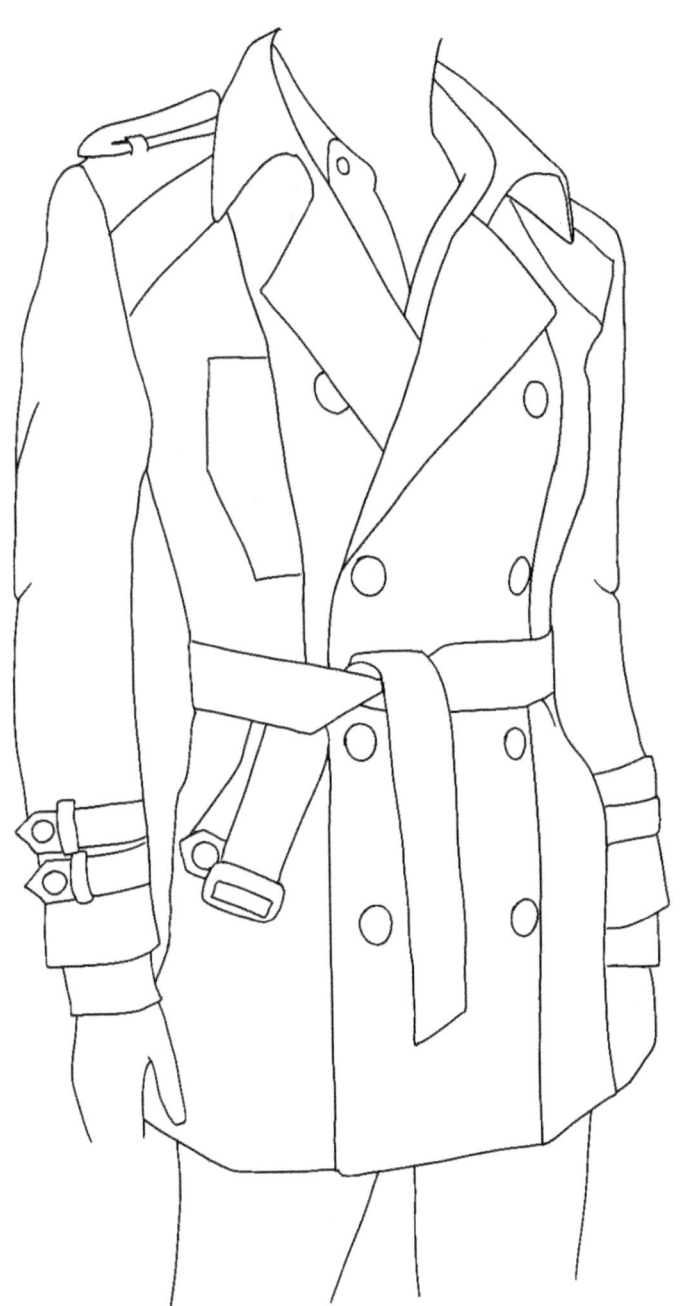

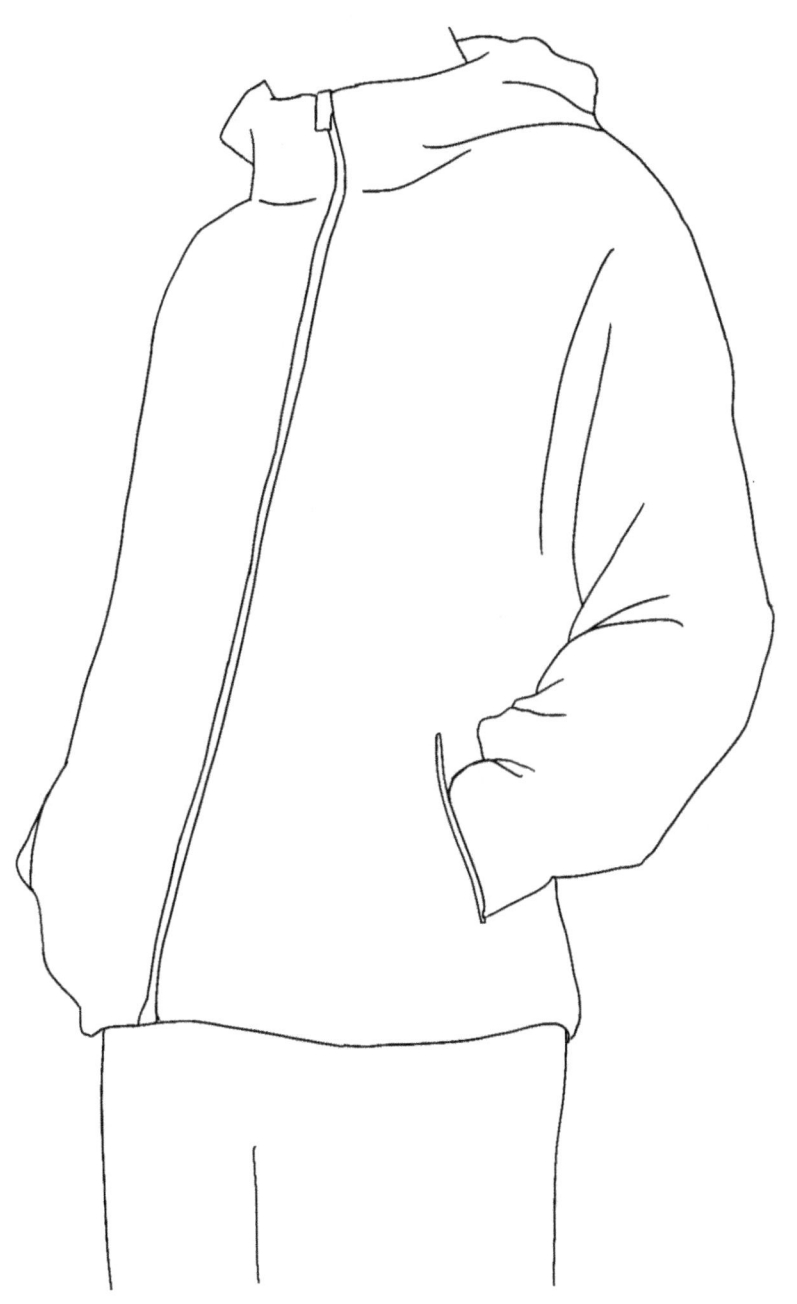

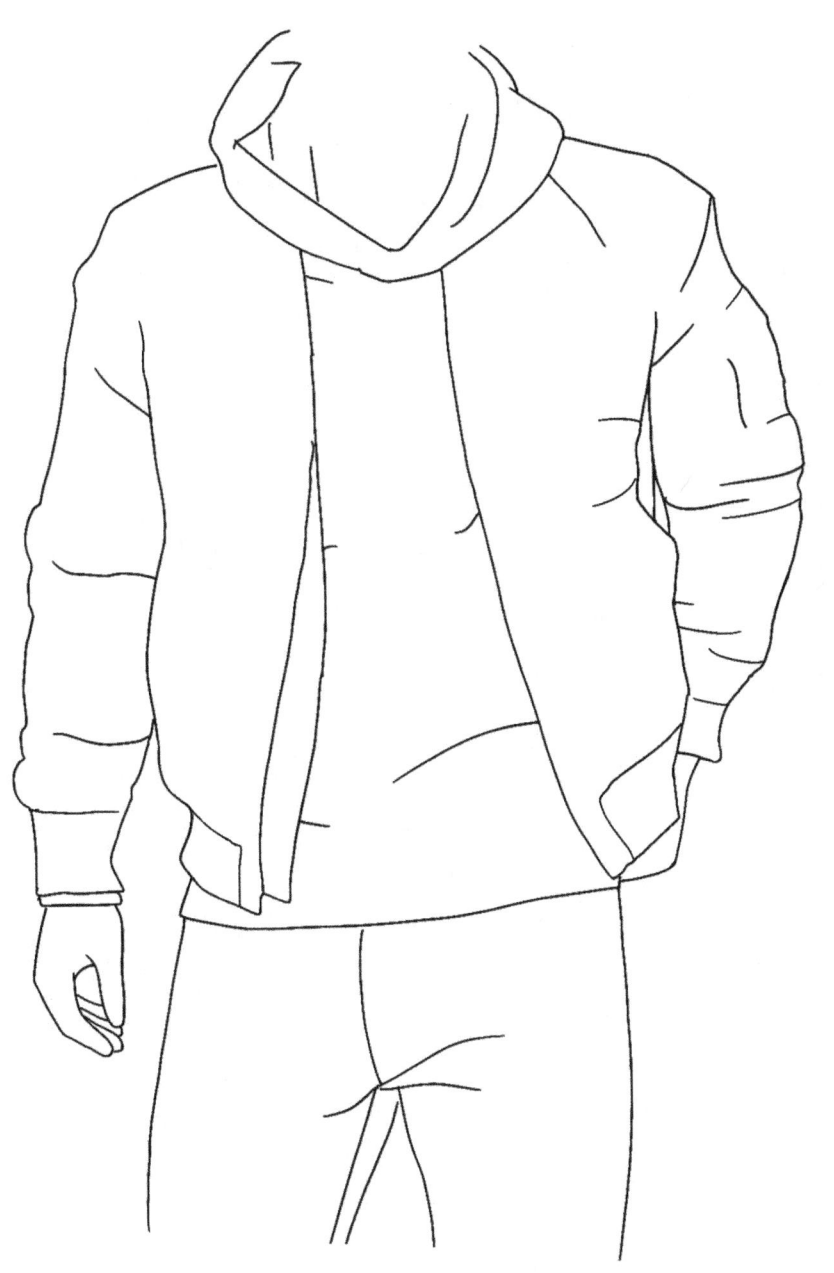

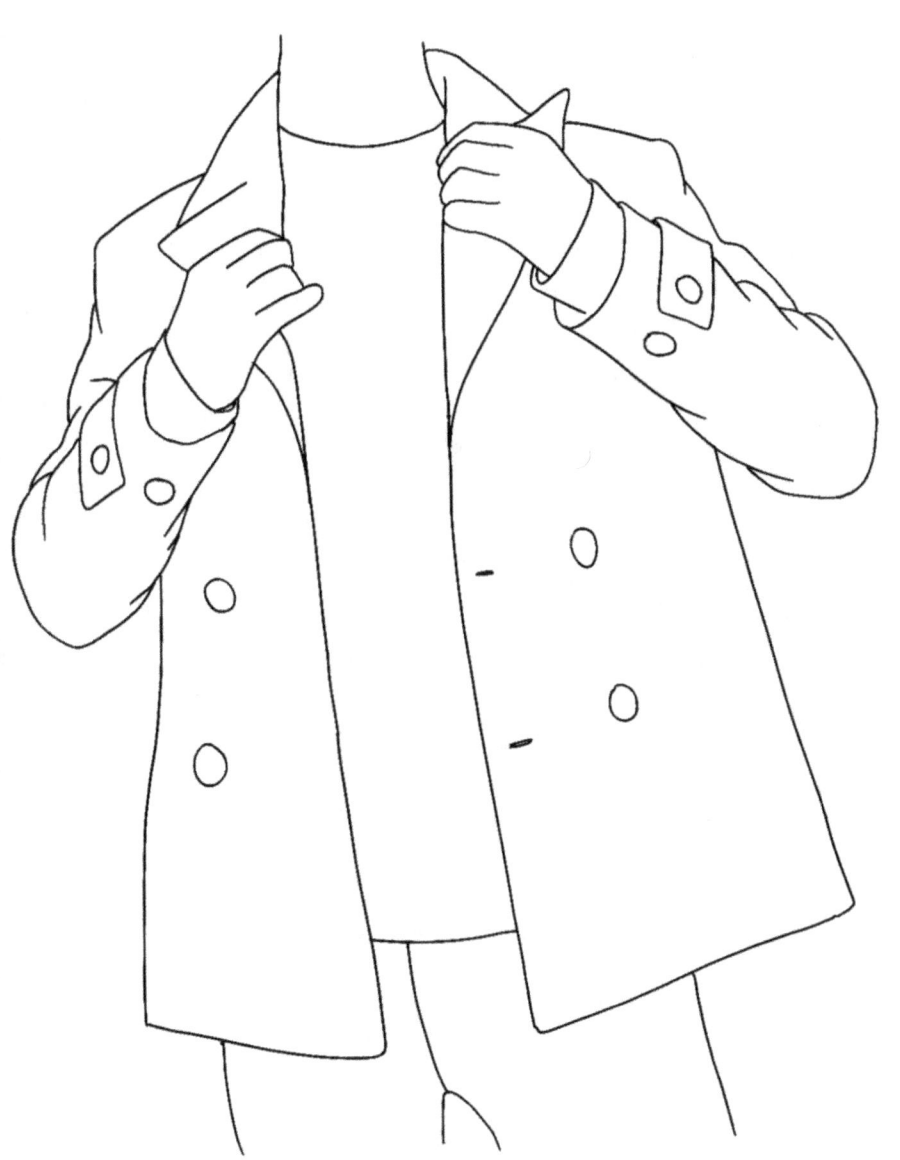

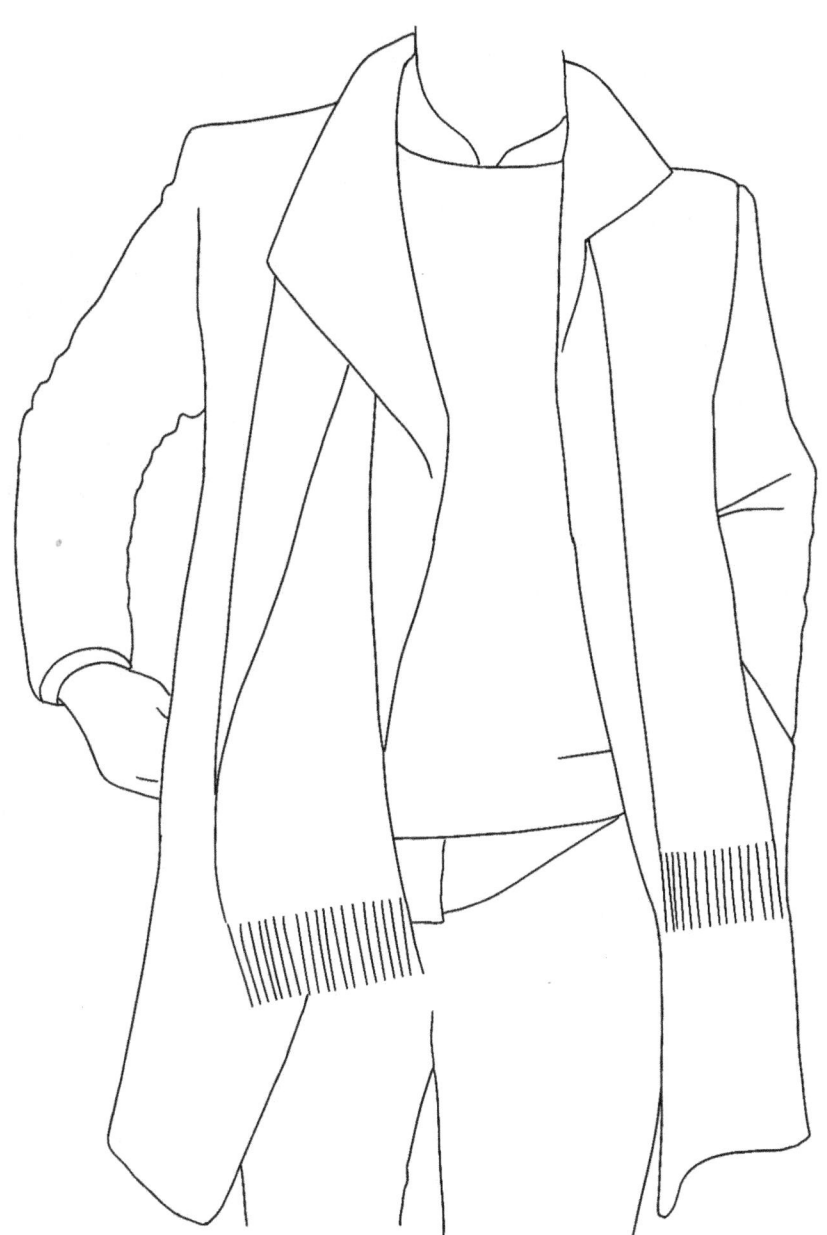

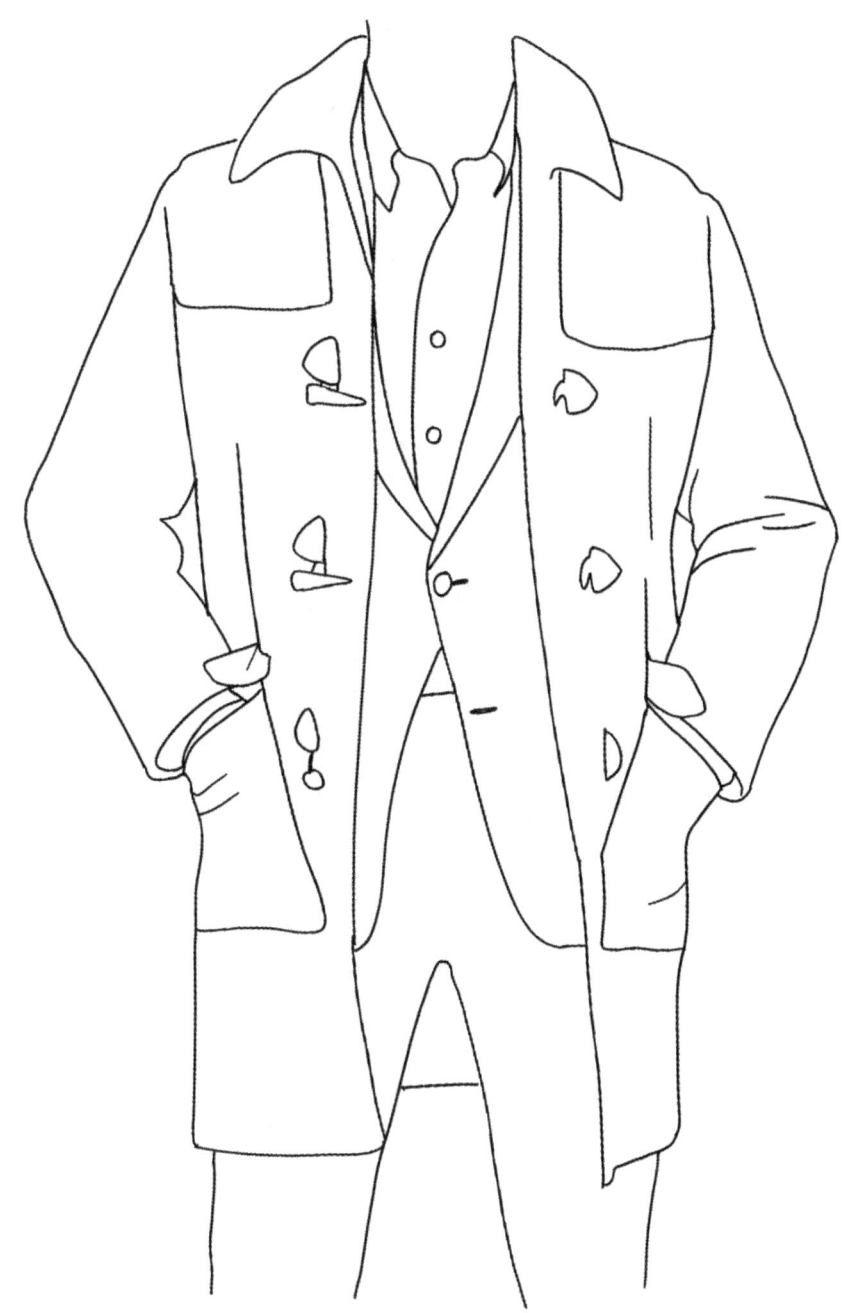

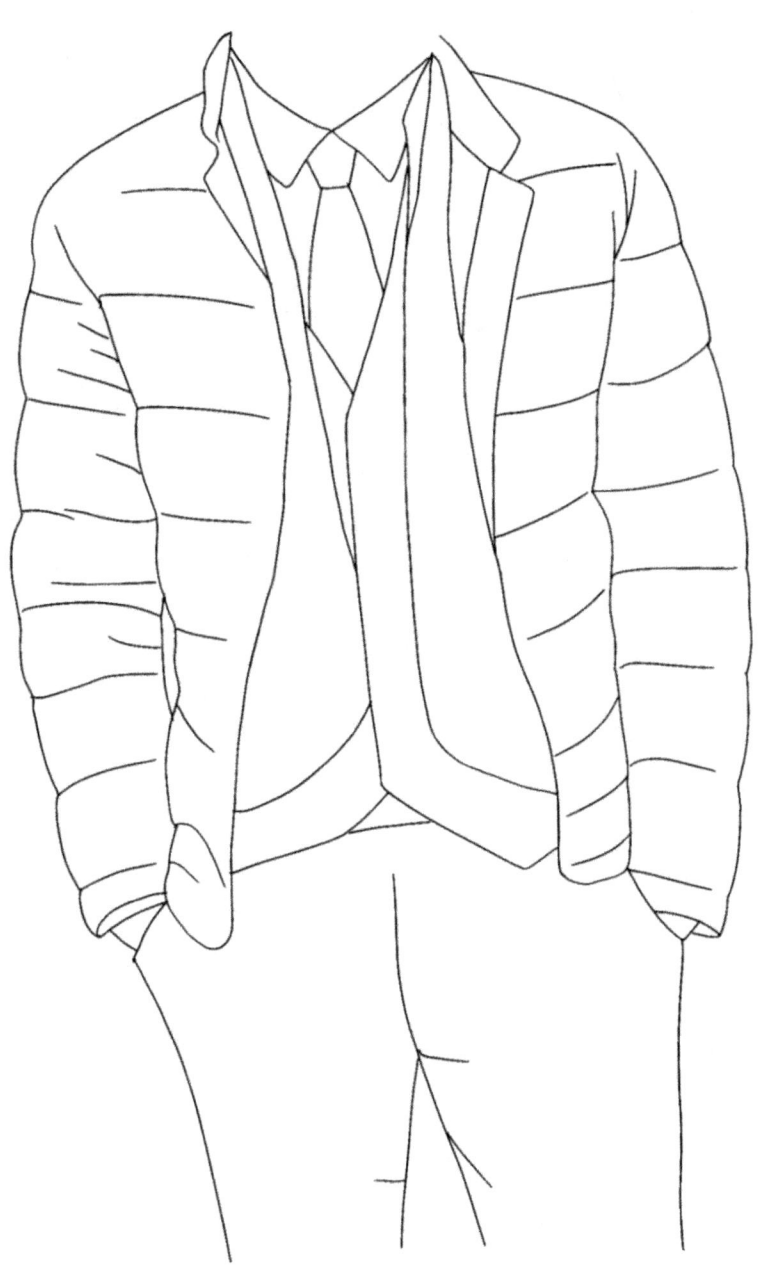

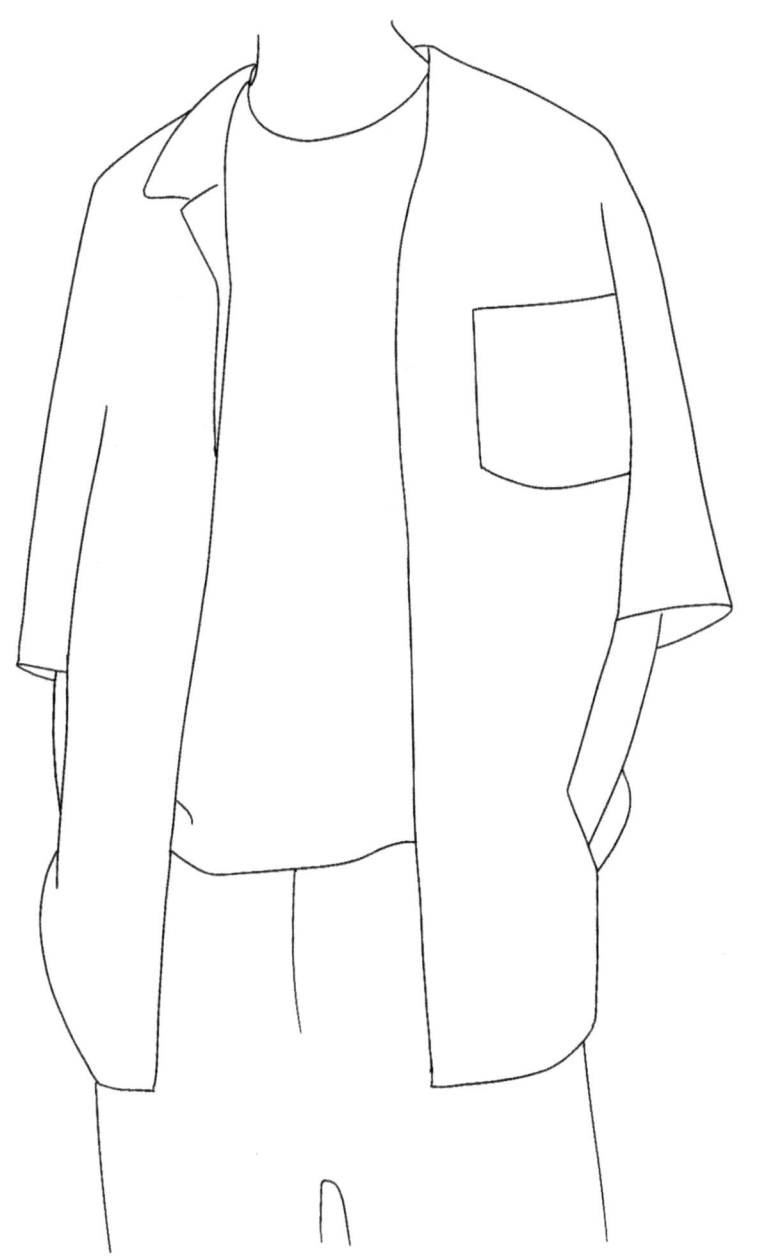

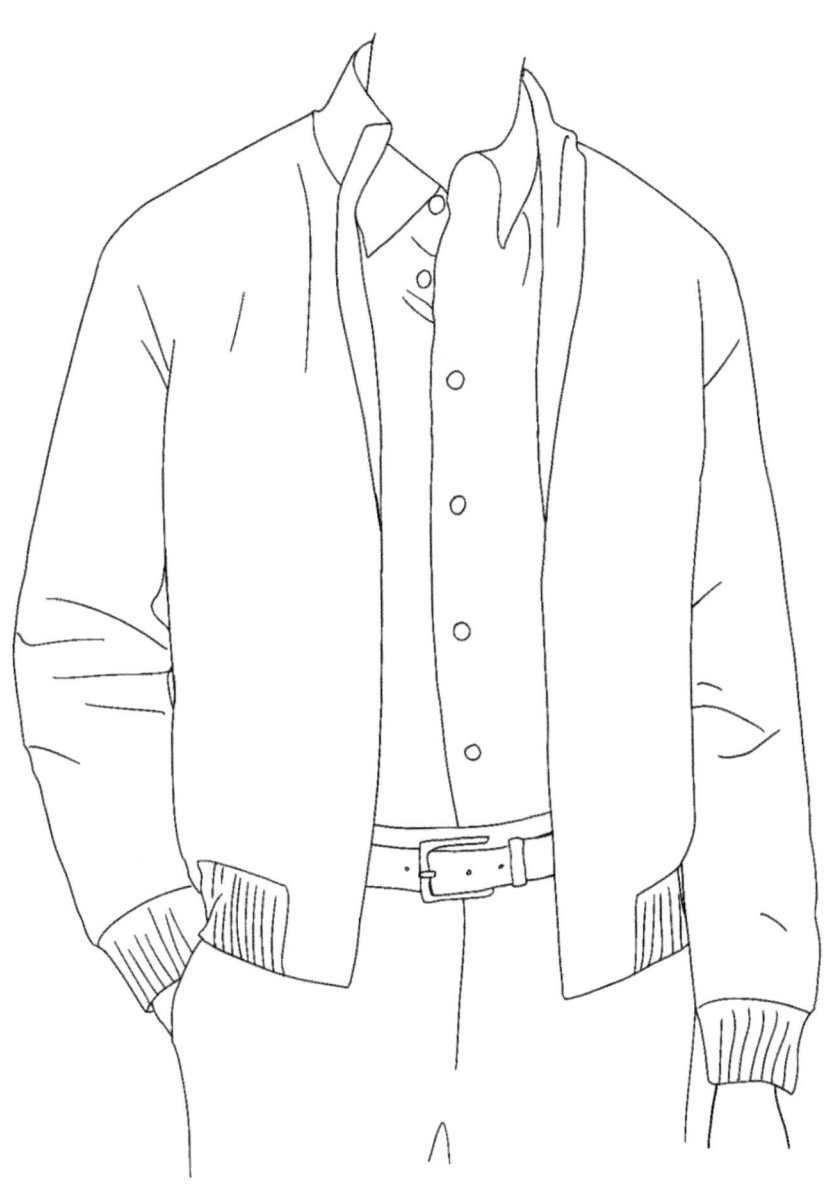

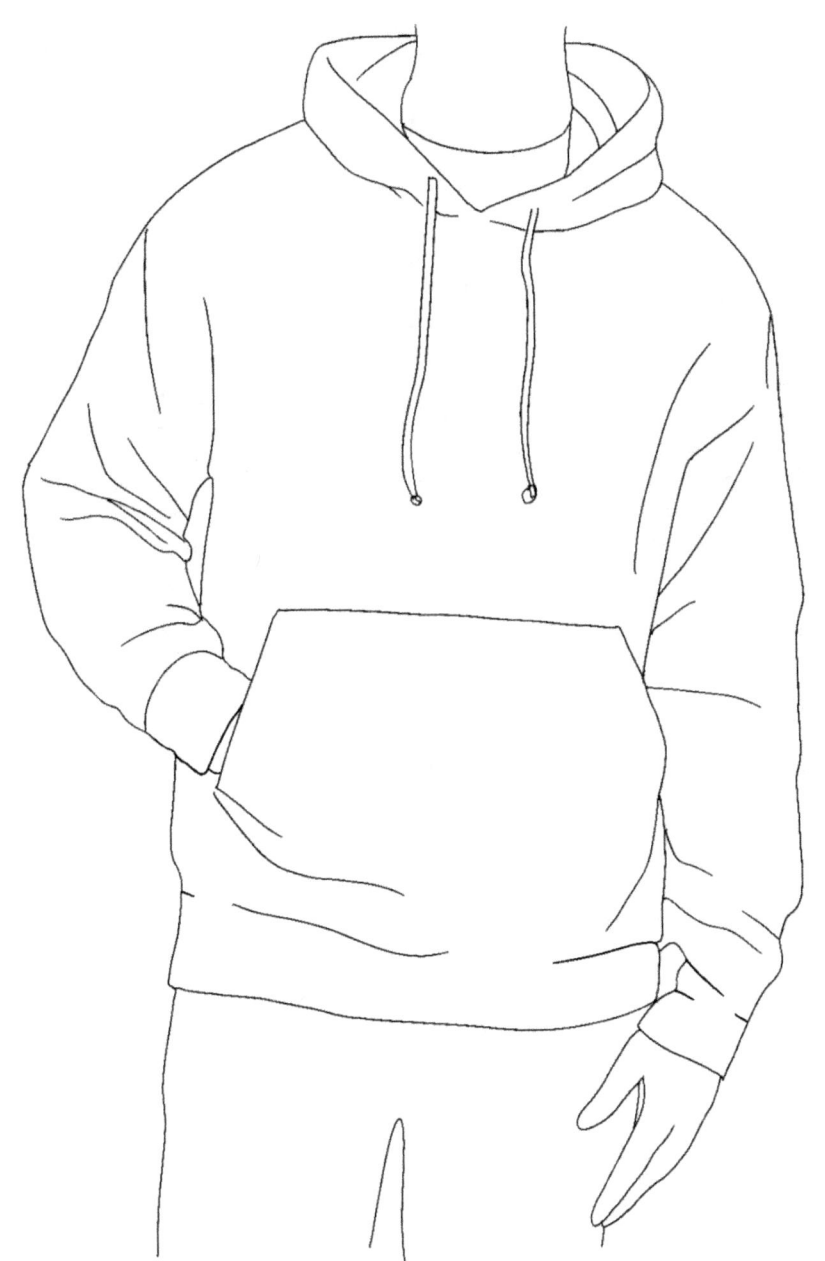

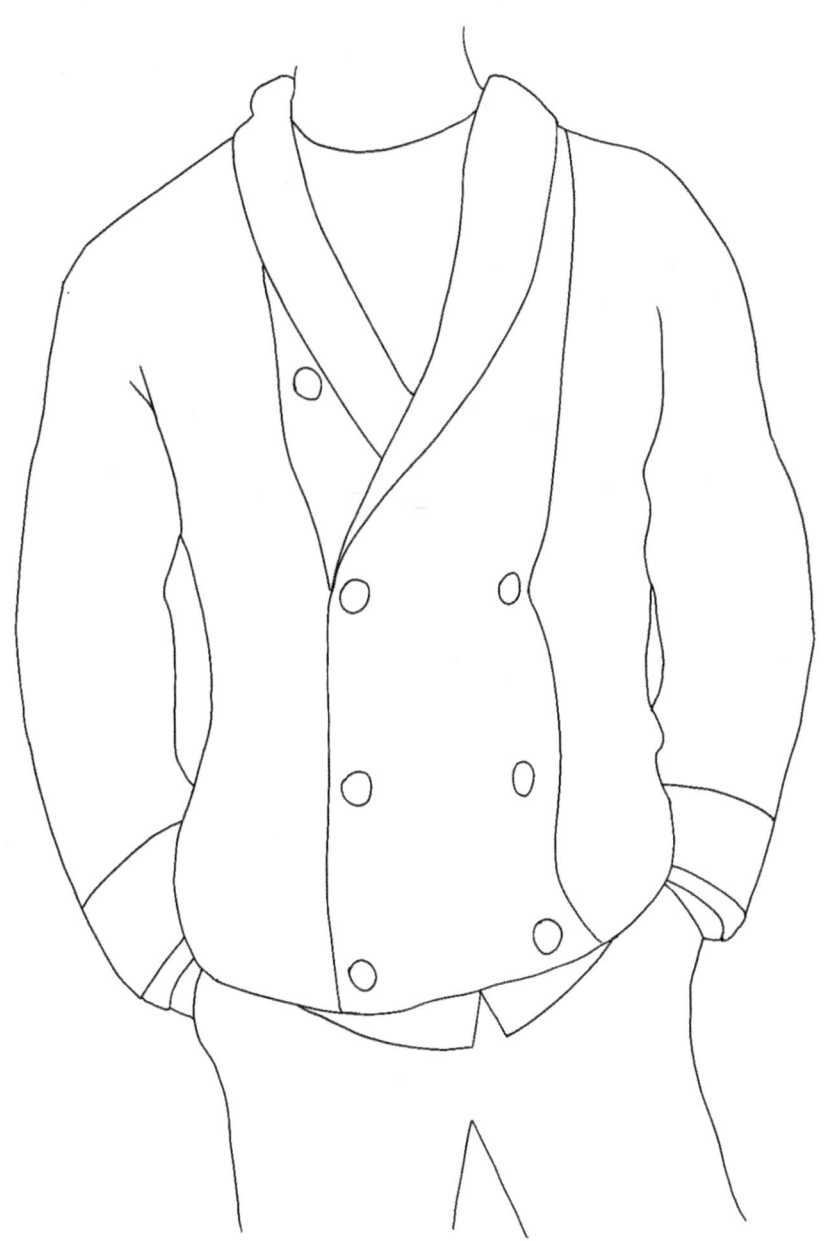

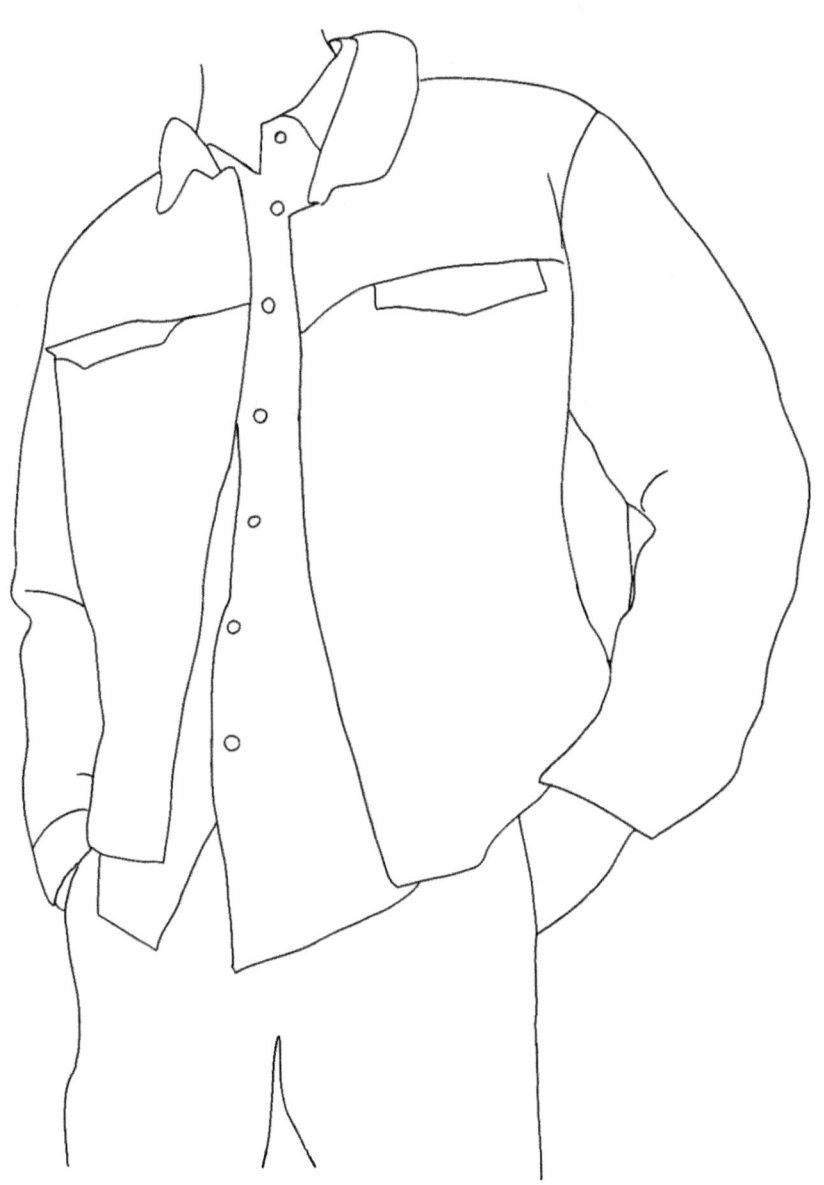

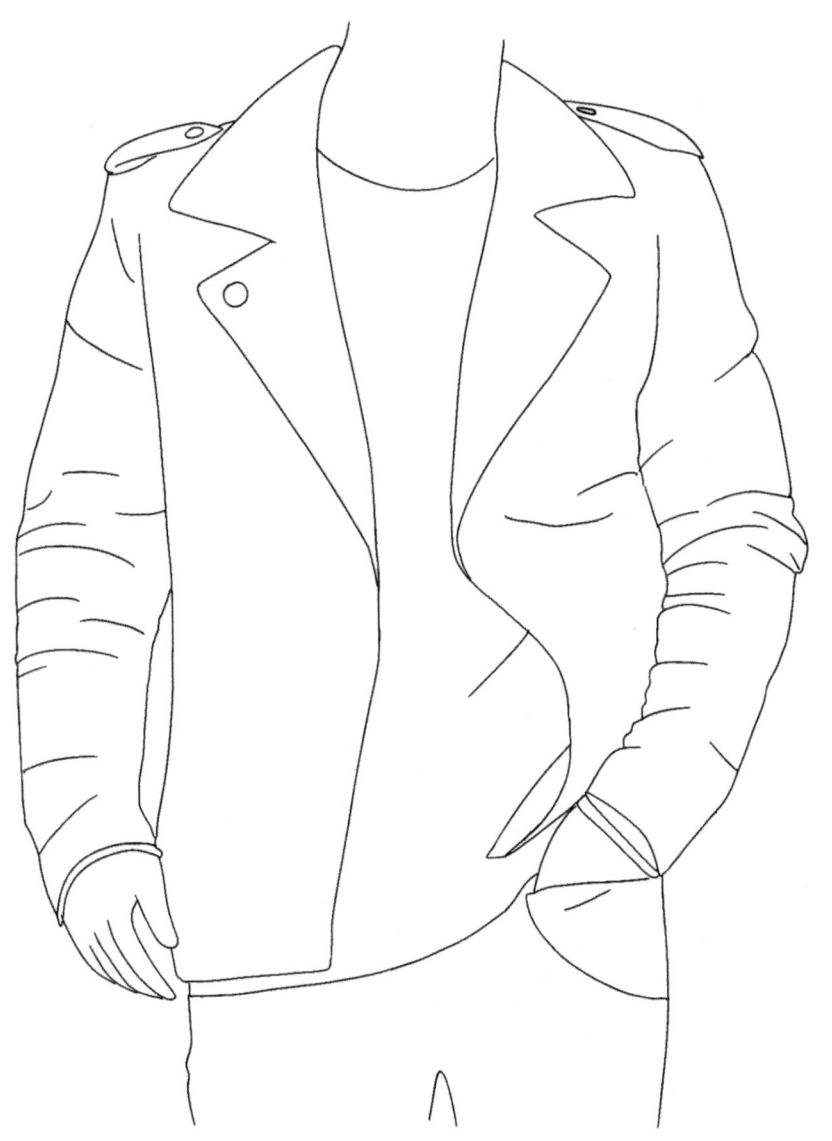

Copyright © 2020 by Noor Almahdi
All rights reserved. No part of this book may be reproduced or used in any manner without written permission from the publisher

ISBN: 9798599934509

Socials
Instagram: @nooralmahdi_art
TikTok: @nooralmahdi_art
YouTube: Noor Almahdi

www.ingramcontent.com/pod-product-compliance
Lightning Source LLC
Chambersburg PA
CBHW070305220526
45465CB00004B/1756